D1484258

Belle Boyd

SIREN OF THE SOUTH

Belle Boyd, 1844-1900

Belle Boyd

Siren of the South

by

RUTH SCARBOROUGH

MERCER UNIVERSITY PRESS
MACON, GEORGIA 31207

Belle Boyd
Siren of the South
by
Ruth Scarborough

© 1997
First paperback edition.
© 1984
Hardback edition.

Mercer University Press
6316 Peake Road
Macon, Georgia 31210-3960

The paper used in this publication meets the minimum requirements
of American National Standard for Information Sciences—
Permanence of Paper for Printed Library Materials, ANSI Z39.48–
1984.

Library of Congress Cataloging-in-Publication Data

Scarborough, Ruth, 1906–
Belle Boyd, siren of the South.
Bibliography: pp. 200
Includes index.
1. Boyd, Bell, 1844–1900. 2 United States—History—
Civil War—1861–1865—Secret Service—Southern States.
3. Spies—Southern States—Biography.
4. Southern States—Biography. I. Title.
E608.B785S28   1983
973.7'86   83–5378

ISBN 0-86554-555-3
MUP/ P164

Dedication

To my good friend
Dr. Sara Helen Cree,
whose patience and understanding
made possible the writing of this book.

A female spy is an engaging creature, but in crinoline
she has an especial, a romantic and absurd, charm.
Belle Boyd, the most famous woman concerned with official
secret activities in the Civil War, not only was enveloped in a cloud
of crinoline, she wore it with grace and elegance. . . .

Joseph Hergesheimer
SWORDS and ROSES

Table of Contents

Illustrations

Preface

AGE 17
Belle Boyd pulls her pistol and kills a
Union soldier who is threatening her mother.

AGE 17
Belle Boyd flirts her way to information
on Union troop movements and carries it
to Stonewall Jackson.

AGE 18
Belle Boyd is imprisoned—
a Confederate spy who gets caught—
and falls in love with her captor.

AND THIS WAS ONLY the beginning of four incredible years in the life of young Belle Boyd!

This spunky West Virginia girl worked among the highest-ranking officers and lowliest foot soldiers of the Civil War, exhibiting an indomitable spirit and loyalty that defied Union authority. This is the factual story of her four years of fame during which she made the Southern cause her own.

As a spy, Belle Boyd was amateurish. Yet, she managed to confuse Union officers and convey truly useful intelligence to Southern military leaders. As a woman, she was not beautiful, but attractive, charming, and personable. She liked the boys in blue as well as those in gray. Most important, she was a sassy spirit just right for her times.

She amassed a provocative collection of titles in the press. Southern papers called her "Joan of Arc of the South," "Siren of the Shenandoah," "Cleopatra of the Secession." The Northern press held a different view: "Camp Follower," "The Most Overrated Spy," "Insincere Courtesan." French newspapers dubbed her "La Belle Rebelle." She probably approved the title!

Belle was a controversial figure in the Shenandoah Valley in the postwar period. Some doubted the authenticity of her story. The dispute was still raging in 1944 when Louis Sigaud published his book, *Belle Boyd, Confederate Spy*. The author was a counterespionage agent in World War I who rose to the rank of Lieutenant Colonel in the Military Intelligence Reserve. His experience augmented his search for the truth about Belle. Using facts from military records, he presented a persuasive case in support of her story. He gave elaborate and dramatic documentation, refuting Belle's detractors, from the *Dictionary of American Biography* and the Social Science Research Council to lesser biographers and pamphleteers.

The present account is based on *Belle Boyd in Camp and Prison*. Belle's emotions as described are taken directly from her book, or occasionally inferred.

Acknowledgments

WRITING THIS BOOK has been hard work and a great pleasure. Much of the enjoyment has come from the spontaneous and generous help I have received from so many people.

Above all, I must credit Mr. Louis A. Sigaud and Dr. Curtis Carroll Davis, whose diligent research and authoritative writings have provided the basis for this work, and all works, on Belle Boyd. The late Mr. Sigaud's 1944 biography, *Belle Boyd, Confederate Spy*, confirmed the authenticity of Belle's own book, *Belle Boyd in Camp and Prison*. Dr. Davis's 1968 reprint of Belle's book, with an excellent introduction and detailed annotation, made Belle's writings available to the contemporary reader. I have extensively quoted or paraphrased both, with the generous permission of Dr. Davis and Mr. John M. Starets, executor of Sigaud's estate.

I could not have accessed Sigaud's notes but for the kindness of Mr. Starets, who led me to them. The notes had found sanctuary in the Bruceton Mills, West Virginia, home of writers George and Kay Evans, who graciously loaned them to me for several exciting evenings of treasure hunting. (The notes are now preserved in the Blennerhassett Island Historical Park Museum, Parkersburg, West Virginia.)

Of invaluable aid were my historical consultants, Laura Virginia Hale of Front Royal, Virginia, Mrs. Stuart Crim of Summit Point, West Virginia, and Mary Ella MacDonald of Martinsburg, West Virginia. I also wish to thank my friends and colleagues, Dr. Millard Bushong and Dr. Gordon Slonaker, both of Shepherd College, Shepherdstown, West Virginia; Mr. and Mrs. Brown Hendricks of Jefferson County, West Virginia; Ruth Seibert of Martinsburg, West Virginia; and Catherine and Alfred Collins of Harpers Ferry, West Virginia, for their help and photography.

Most of my research was done in the Library of Congress in Washington, where, in the Rare Books Section, I found my chief source: Belle Boyd's own account, *Belle Boyd in Camp and Prison.* Other libraries used were the Handley Memorial Library in Winchester and the Samuels Library in Front Royal, Virginia; the West Virginia University Library in Morgantown, Fairmont State College Library in Fairmont, and Shepherd College Library in Shepherdstown, all West Virginia; the McClung Historical Room of the Lawson McGhee Library in Knoxville, Tennessee; and the Main Library of the University of Tennessee.

Many other authors on Belle Boyd were helpful in preparing my book; they are listed in the bibliography.

I wish to express my deep appreciation to my editor, Fred Cree Schroyer; to my typists, Jeanne Schroyer and Ann Cloonan; to my friend Sara Cree (in whose home the book was written); and to members of my family and my friends for their encouragement.

Finally, I wish to thank my friends for their kindness and understanding while I neglected them to concentrate on writing this book. I hope their pleasure in reading it will compensate!

—Ruth Scarborough
Pineview, Georgia

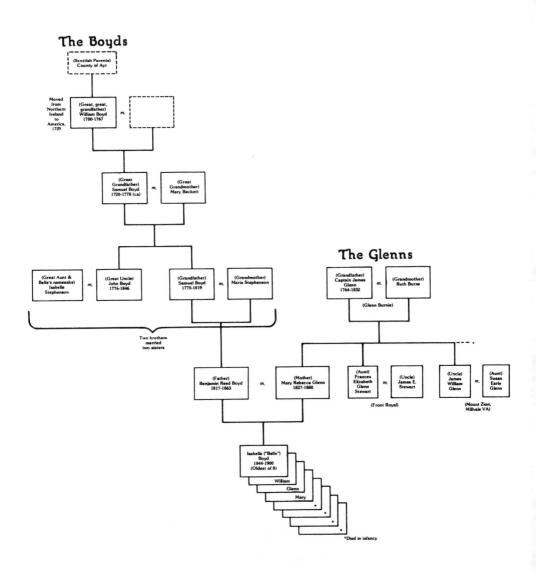

Belle Boyd's ancestry. (Illustration by J. Daniel Barker.)

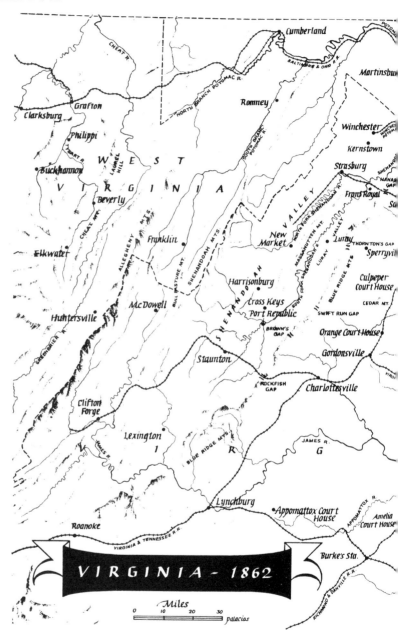

Virginia, 1862, showing the theater of Belle Boyd's Civil War exploits. Many locales mentioned in her story are depicted.

(*Map reproduced from* Terrible Swift Sword, © *1963 by Bruce Catton, by permission of Doubleday and Co., Inc.*)

Martinsburg WV, 1861. This beautifully detailed map shows Belle Boyd's
home town when she was 17. Note
Queen Street and Burke Streek, streets
where Belle lived. It is fascinating to
imagine Belle walking across the Public
Square (the light area where Queen and
King Streets intersect) or riding her
horse Fleeter across the meadows and
dirt roads around town. The Baltimore
and Ohio Railroad, with its depot and
machine shops, built through Martinsburg only a dozen years earlier, curves
from right-center down to bottom-center
of the map; Belle rode this very stretch
of track many times, traveling to
Washington both free and as a prisoner.

This map was used by the Union
army—note, in the lower left corner,
"Approved James W A—Capt U S
Army Dec 1861," and the notations
"Rocky Ridge Commanding Town" and
"Commanding Hight".

Other interesting features are the
cemeteries; park; toll road (top of map);
lime kilns; mills and distillery; the shad-
ing to show topography; and the geology
and soil notations. The map is drawn in
ink on linen.

An oddity of the map: it is oriented
to be read with north to the right,
instead of north at the top. Also,
"Martinsburg" and the scale are upside
down for reasons unknown.

Francis Silver, Berkeley County Sur-
veyor of Lands, Martinsburg WV led the
author to this Map; it is reproduced here
from a negative obtained from the
National Archives (Record Group No.
77, G463-11).

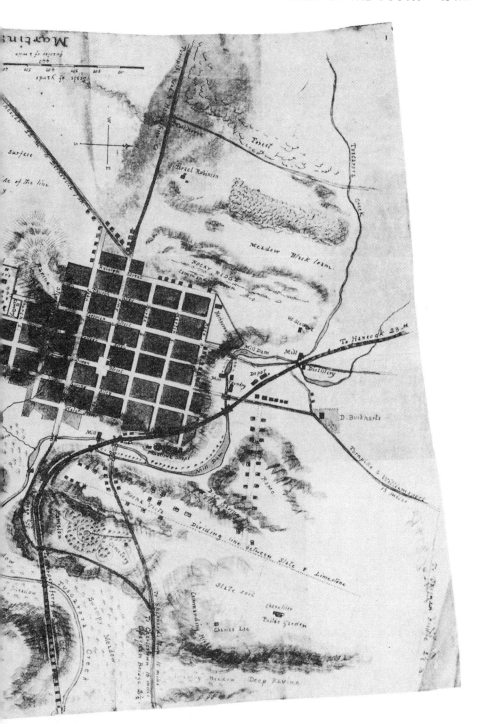

A Spy Is Born

(1844-1862)

From the Boyd family Bible. Under "Births" in the left column, the second entry reads, "Maria Isabella Boyd daughter Benjamin R & Mary R Boyd was born 9th day May 1843. 7 1/2 O.Clock Morning Martinsburg B. County Va". The year 1843 is believed to be an error (see Note 3 for Chapter 1). (Courtesy of Laura Virginia Hale and the Warren Rifles Confederate Museum, both Front Royal VA.)

CHAPTER ONE

Belle of Martinsburg

9 MAY 1844—JUNE 1861

I did not dream how soon my youth
was to be "blasted with a curse" . . .
the curse of civil war.[1]

IN 1844, MARTINSBURG, VIRGINIA was a thriving, sixty-six-year-old community at the northern end of the Shenandoah Valley. It was the county seat of Berkeley County, which two decades hence would join the western Virginia counties to form the state of West Virginia. Only sixty-four miles from Washington, Martinsburg was known as the "Northern Gateway to the Shenandoah."[2]

It was into a quiet home in the peaceful village of Martinsburg that Maria Isabella Boyd was born at 7:30 A.M. on 9 May 1844.[3] "Belle" Boyd would be the first of eight children, the products of a colorful and accomplished lineage.

The lush dairyland of County Ayr in southwestern Scotland spawned the Boyds, who then settled briefly in Northern Ireland, and thence migrated to America. The first to traverse the Atlantic was Belle's great-great-grandfather William Boyd, who arrived in Virginia in 1729. His son Samuel had two sons, John and Samuel, who married two sisters, Maria and Isabella Stephenson. Samuel and Maria had a son, Benjamin Reed Boyd, who fathered Belle. She was named for her grandmother and great aunt.[4]

Belle's mother was Mary Rebecca Glenn, the daughter of Captain James Glenn, who built the beautiful mansion Glenn Burnie in neighboring Jefferson County, Virginia in 1802.[5] Captain Glenn and his wife

Ruth Burns had several children,[6] including Francis Elizabeth who married James Erskine Stewart, a Martinsburg attorney. They lived in Washington for a time but later moved to Front Royal, Virginia, where they would play an important role in Belle's espionage career.

Captain Glenn's only son was James William, who lived in Warren County, Virginia. A noted horseman, he often visited his mother at Glenn Burnie and probably taught Belle her skills in horsemanship.[7]

When Belle was quite young, her family moved to Bunker Hill, a small village ten miles south of Martinsburg. Her father operated a general store and they lived in a comfortable two-story house beside Mill Creek.[8] Belle described it:

> Imagine a bright warm sun shining on a pretty two-storied house, the walls of which are completely hidden by roses and honeysuckle in most luxuriant bloom. At a short distance in front of it flows a broad, clear, rapid stream: around it silver maples wave their graceful branches in the perfume-laden air of the South.[9]

As Belle grew, the world grew around her. When she was five, Martinsburg acquired a railroad roundhouse and shops, becoming a "railroad town" (Baltimore and Ohio line) and gaining rapidly in population.[10] When Belle was eight or ten, Benjamin Boyd moved his store to Martinsburg, erecting a stone building on Queen Street east of the railroad. He moved his family from their rural setting to a home at 126 East Burke Street.[11] He also ran a farm (part of the estate of Glenn Burnie) inherited by Mary Boyd from her father. As Martinsburg expanded, Benjamin Boyd's business prospered, providing the family with enough wealth to live comfortably.[12]

In her own book, *Belle Boyd in Camp and Prison*, Belle reveals a tightly knit family, responsible and protective toward one another. An understanding and friendly man, Ben Boyd was devoted to his family.

Mary Boyd is described by Belle as tall, slender, and outgoing, a woman of great courage, and resolute.[13] Married at sixteen, she had Belle when she was seventeen. Of the eight children of Mary Boyd, four died in infancy (two boys and two girls) and were buried in Green Hill Cemetery in Martinsburg. Belle notes, "I passed my childhood as all happy children usually do, petted and carressed by a father and mother, loving and beloved by brothers and sisters."[14]

Belle spent weeks and even months with her grandmother at Glenn Burnie and often visited her aunt and uncle (the Stewarts), first in Washington, then in Front Royal. The Stewarts' daughter Alice was Belle's age and a favored playmate. Virtually never alone, Belle had a childhood that was a swirl of siblings, aunts, uncles, cousins, and grandparents.[15]

The Boyds were very much a part of the civic, religious, and social life of Martinsburg. They were members of the Martinsburg Presbyterian Church. Mr. Boyd was a member of Masonic Lodge No. 136 in Martinsburg.[16]

Evidently, Belle's indulgent parents attempted to guide and discipline her through love rather than fear or force. This indulgence may have been a key factor in Belle's rapid development as a spirited, mischievous scamp. Belle was dynamic and athletic, becoming an accomplished horsewoman early. She had a reputation as an impulsive tomboy. Louis Sigaud, Belle's first biographer, relates a typical story:

> One day in 1855 Belle's parents entertained some distinguished guests at dinner, but eleven-year-old Belle was not allowed at the table; she was "too young," they said, for such social functions. Everything was perfect: the food, the conversation, the hospitality. Ben and Mary Boyd were smiling at their guests and at each other as gracious compliments were paid them. Then came the time to leave the table and adjourn to the living room.
>
> Abruptly hosts and guests were startled by odd noises just outside; they increased rapidly in volume. The door was thrust open violently and a horse and rider plunged into the dining room, sliding to a halt short of the table. The slim, fair-haired rider sat firmly in the saddle, in perfect command of the prancing white-and-brown-spotted animal. Belle's father moved quickly toward her, and she defiantly looked him in the eye and said, "Well, my horse is old enough, isn't he?"
>
> The Boyds were embarrassed and angry at the behavior of their daughter. The guests, however, were amused and impressed by the reckless assurance and resolute defiance of the young lady. The guest of honor, a high state official,

interceded: "Surely so high a spirit should not be thought-lessly quelled by severe punishment! Mary, won't you tell me more about your little rebel?" (What a prophetic name he used!) As was to happen many times in later years, her resistance to authority was tolerated and punishment was averted.[17]

Her youthful visits around the Shenandoah Valley taught Belle its beauty, geography, and a deep love for the area. As she observed, "There is, perhaps, no tract of country in the world more lovely than the Valley of the Shenandoah."[18] This verdant land between the Blue Ridge and the Allegheny Mountains, cut by the Shenandoah River, would be the seat of her wartime exploits.

The Boyds were typically Southern in their acceptance of slavery. The practice was questioned but tolerated during Colonial times; both George Washington and Thomas Jefferson opposed the system and yet were slaveholders.[19] The original draft of the Declaration of Independence included a clause forbidding slavery, but the convention voted it down, excluding the statement from the final document.[20] Southerners assumed an apologetic attitude until the rise of the abolitionists and the antislavery crusade which placed the South on the defensive.

The cotton trade required cheap labor and consequently fostered a brisk slave trade. In defending the slave system, planters cited history, biblical teachings, ancient philosophers, and economic need. Most slaves lived in the cotton-and-tobacco belt east of the Appalachian Mountains, in the Tidewater and Piedmont region. Few were in the mountainous area or to the west, or in northern Virginia where the Boyds lived. Slavery became a hot issue in 1820 with the Missouri Compromise, which drew a line in the Louisiana Purchase territory beyond which slavery could not expand.[21]

The Boyds' wealth permitted them to have several household slaves, including Eliza Hopewell Corsey, Belle's maid. Although only a few years her senior, Eliza became responsible for Belle's welfare, as well as being her personal servant, bodyguard, and confidante. Her skin was dark brown and she was an alert, fastidious person. Eliza became an essential part of the Boyd household.[22] The mischievous Belle took great delight in shocking Eliza with her youthful pranks and was always rewarded by Eliza's scolding. During the war Eliza would become involved in Belle's espionage activities.

Belle attended school in Martinsburg with her brothers and sister. But when she turned twelve, her parents decided that she should be further educated outside the valley. In a well-meaning effort to make a lady of their tomboy, and in keeping with the Southern tradition of wealthy parents sending their daughters to finishing school, they enrolled young Belle in Mount Washington Female College in the Baltimore suburb of the same name.[23]

Belle entered Mount Washington in 1856, studying French, music, and classical literature.[24] She was surprisingly attentive to her studies, and, not surprisingly, equally attentive to extracurricular activities. Fun-loving and playful, she enjoyed school life. In one notable episode, she and some companions went to the college's Octagonal Room in the main building and carved their initials on a window. Her initials remain there to this day. Now known as Mount Saint Agnes College, the institution is a Catholic school for women.[25]

While Belle was in Baltimore the Boyds moved within the town of Martinsburg, from East Burke Street to 501 South Queen Street. This would be their home throughout the war years.[26] It was a comfortable two-story house in a nice residential area not far from the center of town. Today a plaque marks the site of the building.

As Belle learned the classics at Mount Washington, mighty social forces ominously smoldered around her. In 1857, when Belle was but thirteen years old, the Dred Scott court case was decided—a slave was property, did not have the rights of a United States citizen, and did not become free when taken to a free state or territory. Abolitionists were completely outraged and the proslavery/antislavery lines were drawn ever sharper.[27]

In 1858 (Belle was fourteen), proslavery senator Stephen A. Douglas was reelected in Illinois following the famous Lincoln-Douglas debates. Although Lincoln lost that election, the debates widely publicized his position against the Dred Scott decision and against extending slavery to the territories.[28]

All this was not lost on the girls of Mount Washington Female College. They were young, alert to the world around them, and came from families of some wealth and political power.[29] As Maryland was a border state, girls from both North and South were enrolled;[30] they were generally loyal to their native section. They read the newspapers and argued the pros and cons of slavery. Not surprisingly, Belle held her own in these stormy dormitory debates. She argued expressively and persuasively, never wavering in her loyalty to the South and its institutions. She notes that:

> Slavery, like all other imperfect forms of society will have its day; but the time for its final extinction in the Confederate states of America has not arrived. . . . Meanwhile, which stands in the better position, the helot [slave] of the South, or the "free negro" of the North—the willing slave of a Confederate master, or the reluctant victim of Federal conscription?[31]

In 1859 Belle turned fifteen. That same year the country was alarmed by abolitionist John Brown's violent attack on the government arsenal at Harpers Ferry, only fifteen miles from Belle's hometown of Martinsburg. Brown's purpose was to arm the slaves in the immediate area so they could then fight to free other slaves.[32]

Despite the nation's troubles, life went on. Belle graduated from Mount Washington and eagerly awaited her debut, a social custom of the day that presented a girl to society. A gay debutante, she dreamed of parties, pretty dresses, suitors, and dances. At sixteen, with her mother and Eliza as chaperones, she spent the winter of 1860-1861 in Washington. Since Martinsburg was not faraway by train, they could return home frequently. (Mr. Boyd and grandmother Glenn, now a widow, cared for the younger children.)

Belle depicts the glamor and the glitter:

> In the winter of 1860-61, when I made my first acquaintance with it (Washington), the season was pre-eminently brilliant. The Senate and Congress halls were nightly dignified by the presence of our ablest orators and statesmen; the salons of the wealthy and the talented were filled to overflowing; the theatres were crowded to excess, and for the last time for many years to come the daughters of the North and the South comingled in sisterly love and friendship.[33]

Belle and her mother probably spent much of their time in Washington with the Stewarts (Belle's aunt and uncle). They resided in a huge house, handsomely furnished, and entertained frequently.

Their Southern sympathies were strong and openly expressed. In the looming war they would leave their magnificent home and flee to Front Royal, Virginia.[34]

During this time Belle was often a guest at the home of the Secretary of War, John B. Floyd, a former governor of Virginia, friend of the Boyds and soon to be a Confederate general. There she met other cabinet members, their families, and distinguished heads of state.[35] Much in the center of things, she heard some of the debates in Congress and was surrounded by able men and women of strong viewpoints. She attended the theatre, musical programs, and social and political gatherings. Listening and learning, entertaining and being entertained, she enjoyed her debutante status but with the ever-present consciousness of the political tensions of this critical period.[36]

Belle portrays herself as a friendly, outgoing person with many beaux.[37] It is likely that during this period she met and was courted by Clifford McVay, an attractive young Virginian who would later become a Confederate Lieutenant. They would not see each other again until two years hence—in the Old Capitol Prison, both captives of the North.[38]

Emotions were running high, tension increased, the spirit of compromise receded, the abolitionists were determined that slavery be abolished, and the hotheads of both North and South were aroused. Though eager to continue the pleasures of youth and womanhood, Belle grew inexorably committed in her heart to the cause of the South.

> At sixteen my education was supposed to be completed, and I made my entree into the world in Washington City with all the high hopes and thoughtless joy natural to my time of life. I did not then dream how soon my youth was to be "blasted with a curse"—the worst that can befall man or woman—the curse of civil war.[39]

John Brown was tried, found guilty of treason and murder, and hanged in Charles Town, Virginia, about twelve miles from Martinsburg. He was regarded as a martyr in the North and a murderer in the South. The song, "John Brown's body lies a-mouldering in the grave, but his soul goes marching on," became a Northern theme song and patriotic ballad.[40]

With the election of Lincoln as president in 1860, the consequent secession of South Carolina, the bombardment of Fort Sumter, and Lincoln's call for volunteers, the spirit of war was in the air.[41]

> It was at this exciting crisis that I returned to Martinsburg; and oh! what a striking contrast my native village presented to the scenes I had just left behind in Washington! My winter had been cheered by every kind of amusement and every form of pleasure; my summer was about to be darkened by constant anxiety and heart-rending affliction.[42]

Believing, as most Southerners did, in the sovereignty of the states and the absolute political and moral right of secession, Belle resolved to devote her hands, heart, and life to the sacred cause of freedom. It was this wholehearted passion and devotion to the South that led her to serve the Confederacy, heedless of consequences, with all the energy and skill at her command.

CHAPTER TWO

Just Before
the Storm

JUNE—3 JULY 1861

"And pray, who may you be, Miss?"
My Negro maid answered him, "A rebel lady."
He turned upon his heel, and said
". . . a _____ independent one, at all events."[1]

SOUTH CAROLINA HAD VOTED to secede from the Union on 20 December 1860. The cotton states followed suit, and South Carolina was joined in secession by Mississippi, Alabama, Georgia, Florida, Louisiana, and Texas. These seven states sent delegates to Montgomery, Alabama, where, on 8 February 1861, a new nation was set up—the Confederate States of America.

Virginia seceded on 17 April 1861,[2] only three weeks before Belle's seventeenth birthday. Robert E. Lee of Virginia, "the leader who was to typify the Confederacy,"[3] followed the example of other Southerners by resigning from the U. S. Army and joining the Army of Virginia because he could not draw his sword against his native Virginia.[4]

Since Martinsburg was the "Northern Gateway to the Shenandoah Valley," it was inevitable that fighting would take place there. At the call to arms, the men of the valley responded. The men of Martinsburg flocked into Company D, the 4th company of the 2nd Virginia Infantry. Belle's father was among the first to enlist. At age forty-four, he left his family and business to serve as a private, later joining the Stonewall Brigade under Thomas "Stonewall" Jackson.[5] Says Belle:

> The enthusiasm of the enlistment was adequate to the occasion. Old men, with gray hairs and stooping forms, young

boys, just able to shoulder a musket, strong and weak, rich and poor, rallied around our new standard, actuated by a stern sense of duty, and eager for death or victory.[6]

As John Esten Cooke, noted Virginia novelist and historian, wrote in 1867,

> They were boys and old men; the heirs of ancient names, who had lived in luxury from childhood, and the humblest of the unlettered sons of toil; students and ploughmen, rosy-cheeked urchins and grizzled seniors, old and young, rich and poor; but all were comrades, trained, united, fighting for a common end, and looking with supreme confidence to the man in the dingy gray uniform, with the keen eyes glittering under the yellow-gray cap, who at Manassas was to win for himself and them that immortal name of "Stonewall," cut now with a pen of iron on the imperishable shaft of history.[7]

The women were eager to do their part, nursing the wounded, gathering intelligence, and defying Union troops if their town were occupied. Stonewall Jackson remarked that the women of Winchester were the truest in the South,[8] and surely that compliment applied in many other Southern towns. One Southerner wrote in 1861 that never "in any age or country, was there ever witnessed such an intense war spirit as that now prevailing among the women of the Confederate States."[9] While the men fought, the women worked to provide arms, equipment, and medicines. Belle was prominent among those who raised funds to this end.[10]

The attractive young Belle was now a grown woman physically and mentally. At seventeen she was a year older than her mother had been when she married. She considered herself an adult, ready to take on the world. From contemporary descriptions and the handful of likenesses that survive her, one can assemble her portrait: a tall, slim, well-proportioned young woman, physically agile and strong; an energetic, charming talker of well-read intelligence; a romantic, sometimes theatrical spirit, usually merry and fun-loving but capable of embers, sparks, and flames.

She loved riding and dancing. Her soft, vibrant voice and merry laugh seldom surrendered control in a conversation, nor did her femininity which she mastered as a tool for manipulating the other sex.

Belle dressed fashionably and tastefully, her figure well adapted to the tightly fitted basque waists of the day, arousing at once male interest and female envy. Her wide, long skirts reached down to the floor, buoyed by the multiple petticoats underneath. Her dark reddish hair typically was wound in a ball at the nape of her neck. Above all, her brown eyes commanded the attention of everyone.[11]

With all these blessings, her face was not what could be called beautiful; but her presence as a whole was beguiling and appealing. In the words of historian John Bakeless:

> The fact is Belle Boyd was one of those girls who don't have to be pretty. She had a way with men, especially young men, in uniform, who became her willing slaves at a glance or, at most, after a very few glances—a situation most convenient for a lady spy.[12]

Belle saw no reason for conforming to the rigid, conventional behavior of young ladies of her day. While she did not deviate from the moral code of her generation, she freely violated common social restrictions. For example, she shocked her more conservative friends by waving to soldiers in the streets, Confederate and Union alike. She walked the streets unchaperoned when she could escape her maid Eliza.[13]

When war came she shocked her contemporaries even more by visiting the military camps, calling on generals and colonels in their tents, and accepting rides with enemy officers and soldiers. Dancing and flirting with Northerners and Southerners alike, she claimed that she had to be on good terms with both sides to gather information. She flirted with the Yankees, assuring them that she lacked ulterior motives, while obtaining military secrets. At times cunning, at other times naive, she was in fact both. Her total lack of self-consciousness around men no doubt occasioned the jealousy of other women.[14] "She was attractive in manner and appearance and of magnetic personality. She possessed dash, energy, courage. . . ."[15]

In the spring of 1861, Belle, her mother, and Eliza returned to Martinsburg from their winter in Washington. As the train moved through the countryside, pausing at every station, she saw signs of spring—the blooming apple trees, the green meadows, the activity at each stop. She no doubt yearned for her comfortable home in Martinsburg, for the parlor filled with Boyd and Glenn furnishings, and for friends and neighbors well remembered. Her family awaited her: her father, her gay and talkative sister Mary, and her young brothers Glenn (eleven) and Will (twelve) with their boyish concerns.

On arriving in Martinsburg, Belle was astonished to learn that her father had enlisted as a private:

> My father was one of the first to volunteer. He was offered that grade in the army to which his social position entitled him; but, like many of our Virginia gentlemen, he preferred to enlist in the ranks, thereby leaving the pay and emoluments of an officer's commission to some others, whose means were not so ample, and whose family might be straitened in his absence from home, an absence that must, of course, interfere with his avocation or profession.[16]

Henry Kyd Douglas, a friend of Belle's and author of *I Rode With Stonewall* [Jackson], also enlisted as a private even though he could easily have obtained a much higher rank. According to Douglas the lower ranks were filled with the best blood of Virginia.[17]

In a few days Ben Boyd's regiment left Martinsburg for a Confederate camp at Harpers Ferry, Virginia, for organization, training, planning, and waiting to see where the Union forces would strike.[18]

At Harpers Ferry, there is a gap in the mountainous Blue Ridge where the Shenandoah River flows into the Potomac. It was the view from this point that Thomas Jefferson said was "worth a voyage across the Atlantic." The confluence of these two rivers and the large bridge that crossed the Potomac, connecting Maryland and Virginia, created a strategic point for commerce, transportation, and military control. Also, Harpers Ferry had one of the largest arsenals in the South.[19] Thus Harpers Ferry was an inevitable attack point where Union troops could cross the river into Virginia. Accordingly, one of the regiments of the Stonewall Brigade was assembled there to defend the crossing. It was in this brigade that Belle's father served, only fifteen miles from their Martinsburg home.

At the departure of Ben Boyd's regiment from Martinsburg there was desolation and depression in the Boyd household. Mrs. Boyd had not been separated from her husband for any significant period of time since their marriage. She sought relief in domestic duties, while Belle turned to her books, making gifts for her father, amusing the children and helping them with their lessons, teasing Eliza, and visiting.[20]

Belle soon grew tired of these activities and, as always, wanted something more exciting. The war seemed far away and she yearned to be a part of the military activities. Why not visit the camp at Harpers Ferry? She knew other wives and daughters were restless too, so why not collect a group and visit the camp?

Belle quickly assembled an entourage and departed for Harpers Ferry. Upon arriving the visitors were surprised to find the camp lively, with officers and men as gay and joyous as though no bloody strife awaited them. The women, again in the society of their menfolk, cast away their anxieties and enjoyed the pleasures of the day, forgetting temporarily the ominous future.[21]

At the impromptu parties and dances, young daughters met young soldiers and ephemeral romances bloomed; many fond vows were exchanged and true hearts pledged. Noted Henry Kyd Douglas, "Mothers and sisters and other dear girls came constantly to Harpers Ferry and there was little difficulty in seeing them. Nothing was serious yet; everything was much like a joke."[22]

But the jubilant mood lasted briefly, as news arrived of advancing Union troops. A Federal army under Major General Robert Patterson was approaching. Ben Boyd's regiment scurried to prepare for battle and Belle and her mother returned to Martinsburg.

General Stonewall Jackson was ready to check any aggressive Union movement and thus encamped at a natural defensive point, Falling Waters on the Potomac River, eight miles north of Martinsburg.[23] The Potomac forms the southern boundary of Maryland (a border state that did not secede) and Falling Waters was on the Virginia (now West Virginia) side of the river.

On 2 July 1861, General Patterson crossed the river at Williamsport, a few miles north of Falling Waters; he advanced toward Martinsburg in an effort to gain control of the northern end of the Shenandoah. On 3 July Belle's father and the rest of Jackson's outnumbered troops retreated through Martinsburg, followed by their protective cavalry under the command of Colonel Turner Ashby. On their heels came the triumphant Federal army, 25,000 strong, marching through Martinsburg with flags flying and bayonets gleaming.[24] It was an unhappy sight for the people of Martinsburg, but one that would be repeated many times before the agony of war was over.

Geography made the Shenandoah Valley a natural focal point in this saddest of all wars. There were at least 112 military engagements in the valley. No other town changed hands as often during the war as Winchester, south of Martinsburg. The least number determined by historians is sixty-eight transfers between the opposing forces. No other town or city was so battered by the effects of the war, except Richmond and Atlanta. The struggle for the Shenandoah Valley made it "the Flanders of America."[25]

On this very first day of Federal occupation, Belle and Eliza had joined other women at a temporary hospital and were taking care of rebel soldiers stricken with fever. As Belle stood close by one of her patients, who was raving in a violent fit of delirium, she was startled by heavy footsteps behind her. Turning quickly, she confronted a captain of Federal infantry, accompanied by two soldiers. The captain held a Federal flag, which he proceeded to wave over the beds of the sick men, calling them "____ Rebels."

Scornfully, Belle retorted, "Sir, these men are as helpless as babies and have, as you may see, no power to reply to your insults."

"And pray, who may you be, Miss?" replied the captain. Belle did not deign to reply, but Eliza, her jaw fixed in anger, indignation glinting in her eyes, spoke for Belle: "A rebel lady!"

The captain then turned on his heel and muttered as he left, "A ____ independent one, at all events."[26]

Later the patients were removed on litters to a quieter and safer place. While they were being moved, some Federal soldiers crowded around and threatened to bayonet the helpless invalids. According to Belle:

> Their gesticulations and language grew so violent; their countenances, inflamed by drink and hatred, were so frightful, that I nerved myself to seek out an officer and appeal to his sense of military honor, even if the voice of mercy were silent in his breast. Let me do him the justice to say, he restrained his turbulent men from further molestation, and I had the unspeakable satisfaction of conveying my sick men to a place of safety.[27]

Belle never forgot the incident, always fearing that her father might, at some time, be the victim of such insults and brutality.

Stimulated by that fear, what had been a firm resolution to serve the South now became an obsession.

July 4th
Fireworks

4-20 JULY 1861

All our male relatives being with the army,
we ladies were obliged to go armed in order to protect
ourselves as best we might from insult and outrage.[1]

THE FOURTH OF JULY 1861—Independence Day in Martinsburg—a holiday for the Federal troops. The Union was eighty-five years old and the Confederacy was barely five months old. Union forces were in undisputed possession of Martinsburg and their troops were celebrating. Regiments paraded and bands played "Yankee Doodle" and other patriotic songs that bright, sunny morning. Whiskey flowed freely; some of the soldiers became drunk, and some arrogant. In this setting small quarrels and fights escalated into rioting. Shots were fired through windows, property was destroyed, and furniture was hurled from homes. Officers tried in vain to restrain the soldiers and stop the tumult.[2]

On that hot and humid day, word spread among the Federals that Belle's bedroom was decorated with rebel flags. A few soldiers, roaring drunk and belligerent, invaded the Boyd home, pushing up the stairs toward Belle's room to destroy the flags. When they reached her room, there was not a rebel flag in sight. Eliza had seen them coming, retrieved the flags, and burned them before they could be desecrated in the enemy's hands.

Not content to stop there, the troops tried to hoist a Union flag over the house to indicate submission to Federal authority. Enough was enough, and Belle's mother interceded. Belle watched from the stairway as one drunken soldier thrust himself in front of her mother. Mary Boyd moved toward the man, saying quietly and resolutely, "Men, every member of my household will die before that flag shall be raised over us."

The soldier cursed her "in language as offensive as it is possible to conceive." And upon that, without hesitating, Belle abruptly ended the encounter. As she later recalled, "I could stand it no longer. My indignation was aroused beyond my control. My blood was literally boiling in my veins. I drew out my pistol and shot him."

The soldier fell and lay motionless. Stunned and horrified, Mary Boyd and Eliza stared at the man, then at Belle. The entire room, instantly sobered, was silent for a moment. Then pandemonium erupted, some soldiers yelling, "Burn the house!" A few bolted from the room to report the shooting to Union headquarters, just down the street. The remaining soldiers shouldered their fallen comrade. "He was carried away mortally wounded, and soon after expired."[3]

Private Frederick Martin of Company K, 7th Pennsylvania Volunteers, was buried in Martinsburg on 7 July; he is thought to be the man Belle killed on 4 July.[4]

Most of the soldiers left the Boyd home immediately after the shooting, but a vengeful few lingered, hastily piling rubbish against the house to burn it. A Boyd servant soon discovered them in the act and rushed into the house. "Oh Missus, Missus, dere gwine to burn de house down. Dere pilin' de stuff ag'in it."[5] Belle immediately sent a servant to Federal headquarters for help, which fortunately arrived before further damage was done.

Belle may have been shocked and shaken, yet she later wrote:

> Shall I be ashamed to confess that I recall without one shadow of remorse the act by which I saved my mother from insult, perhaps from death—that the blood I then shed has left no stain on my soul, imposed no burden upon my conscience?[6]

News soon reached her father that Belle had shot a Union soldier, followed by a false report that she had been jailed. Her father was at a Confederate camp in Darkesville, near Martinsburg. There was an immediate clamor that she be rescued and some soldiers volunteered to storm her prison. A general furor prevailed, for their homes had been threatened and entered, and their women had been insulted.

Fortunately, more accurate information reached the camp, ending plans to rescue Belle.[7]

Characteristically, Belle was amused by the false rumor, pleased by the reaction of the soldiers, and glad that no violence followed:

> It is with pride and gratitude that I record this proof of their esteem and respect for what I had done. It is with no less pleasure I reflect that their devotion was not put to the test, and that no blood was shed on my account.[8]

At Federal headquarters in Martinsburg there was great excitement and indignation. The officer in charge, accompanied by several of his staff, promptly called at the Boyd home to investigate the affair. Witnesses to the shooting were thoroughly questioned, including Mary Boyd, Eliza, and Belle. Each gave her version of the incident. The anxious women then waited in tense silence. The officers finally gave their conclusion: Belle should be acquitted; she "had done perfectly right." To avoid further trouble sentries were posted around the Boyd house and Federal officers visited there daily as an additional precaution.[9]

The fact that the Federals allowed the shooting of one of their soldiers to go unpunished seems incredible, but Washington was then practicing appeasement. The border states (Maryland, Delaware, Missouri, and Kentucky) had not seceded and Lincoln did not want to anger them; keeping them in the Union was essential. It is likely that he instructed his generals to treat the rebels leniently and avoid bloodshed.[10]

How far the North would go in appeasing the South is shown by Federal action toward another noted rebel spy, Washington's Rose O'Neil Greenhow, aunt of Mrs. Stephen A. Douglas, the senator from Illinois. When she was detected transmitting information to the Confederates that led to victory in the first battle of Manassas (Bull Run), she was imprisoned. After a few months she was released and sent south, with the single stipulation that she must confine her activities within the Confederacy and not return north of the Potomac.[11]

Belle soon learned that exoneration did not mean freedom. The Boyd house was carefully guarded by sentries, as planned. But, realizing that Belle was a potential troublemaker, the sentries had a second purpose: to watch her carefully. Undaunted by their watchfulness, she began to profit from her enforced acquaintance with the enemy. It was an opportunity that "the Rebel Spy did not fail to turn to account on many occasions."[12] By chatting and flirting with her Northern sentries, she learned of troop positions and plans. Carefully committing this intelligence to paper, she sent it by trusty messengers to Confederate officers. Foremost among her trusty messengers was Eliza.[13]

Belle was handicapped by her lack of training in the art of transmitting military intelligence. She simply wrote messages in her own hand and forwarded them. She was successful for a time, but one of her messages, through accident or treachery, fell into enemy hands. It was written in longhand and signed by Belle.[14]

And so, less than a week after the 4 July shooting, Belle was summoned to Federal headquarters, ushered into the office of an exceedingly angry colonel, and confronted with the intercepted message. Her offense was a very serious one, he thundered; threats and reprimands followed. Solemnly and significantly he read an article of war to Belle:

> Whoever shall give food, ammunition, information to, or aid and abet the enemies of the United States government in any manner whatsoever, shall suffer death, or whatever penalty the honorable members of the court-martial shall see fit to inflict.[15]

Belle listened quietly, coldly, and unfrightened. The words sounded terrifying, but she knew it was a warning, not a formal action or court-martial. An awkward pause followed. Finally she rose to her feet, and made a low bow with the comment, "Thank you, gentlemen of the jury."[16] Although the colonel must have found galling Belle's stubborn refusal to be repentant or intimidated, he dismissed her. She departed angry and rebellious, knowing that from this time forward she would be a suspect and blamed for any mischief that occurred. Her rebel heart afire, she left Union headquarters, indulging in dark schemes of retaliation. But her vengeance would not be quelled in a solitary event; it would rather be achieved through relentless intelligence action against the North.[17]

The furor over Belle's deeds in Martinsburg gradually subsided as military activities increased in the east toward Washington. The Boyd home became less carefully watched as Federal troops were withdrawn. Still, Belle's parents decided that she would be safer with her aunt and uncle (the Stewarts) in Front Royal, and Belle headed south with a light heart, happily ignorant of the fact that she would be in even more dangerous territory.[18]

CHAPTER FOUR

Nurse
and Courier

21 JULY—AUTUMN 1861

. . . my duties were painful in the extreme;
but . . . I allowed but one thought to keep possession
of my mind . . . I was doing all a woman
could do in her country's cause.[1]

CONFIDENT OF ITS MILITARY might, the South naively expected a war of short duration. It was a common remark that "one Southerner could lick at least four Yankees."[2] Moreover, some of the Union's best officers, many of whom were West Point graduates, had sided with their states in the Confederacy.[3]

Because the border state of Maryland was divided, with part of the population notoriously hostile to the Union, troops were amassed in Washington. They remained without major movement until mid-summer. By that time the North had grown impatient and popular opinion demanded an attack on the Confederacy. "On, on to Richmond!" was the cry.[4]

Southern forces under General P. G. T. Beauregard were a mere twenty-five miles across the Potomac from Washington at Manassas Junction. Another Confederate force under General Joseph E. Johnston moved from the Shenandoah Valley to join Beauregard's troops, doubling the threat to the capital. Thus the battle lines were drawn for what would be the first of two battles at Manassas, along a muddy little stream called Bull Run.[5]

The Battle of Manassas was fought on 21 July 1861, only seventeen days after Belle killed the Yankee soldier in her home. Folks from Washington, who expected an easy Union victory, came on horseback and in carriages to witness the fight. Carrying picnic lunches, they congregated on hillsides overlooking Bull Run to get a good view of the expected Southern defeat.

By three o'clock in the afternoon it appeared that the Union had won an easy victory. However, the arrival of a fresh detachment of Johnston's army enabled the Confederates to turn the tide and the Federal forces broke and ran. A rallying cry from General Bee gave General Thomas Jackson his famous nickname: "Look! There is Jackson, standing like a stone wall! Rally behind the Virginians!"[6]

Federal troops, plunged into hopeless confusion, were unable to obey command. Thousands broke rank and scurried toward Washington, abandoning arms, their own wounded, and their prisoners. Soldiers became mixed with sightseers, and a U. S. congressman, Alfred Ely of New York, was taken prisoner by the Southerners! What had been an army became a panic-stricken mob; what should have been an orderly retreat became a disorderly flight. Some Union troops stopped when they reached their fortifications on the Potomac, but most crossed the river into Washington.[7]

The Battle of Manassas taught the North that the South would not be easily subdued and the Federals prepared for a long, hard struggle to restore the Union. Unfortunately for the South, the battle made them overconfident and hopeful of quick victory, underrating the strength and determination of the North. "The Confederates were insane with joy, celebrating from one end of the country to the other."[8] For the South it was the high tide of devotion and pride: one more victorious battle and the Yanks would be defeated! Confederate troops could then return to their wives and families.

Intoxicated with enthusiasm and excitement, young men hastened to enlist before the war should end. Every community saw men drilling, marching, shooting; the women hastily sewed uniforms and knitted scarves and socks. "War weddings" proliferated.[9]

Belle was happily ensconced in the home of her aunt and uncle, the Stewarts in Front Royal, where they had taken refuge from Washington (their beautiful home there had been confiscated and converted into military barracks). Belle loved this charming Shenandoah Valley community:

> I wish it were in my power to give my readers some faint idea
> of this picturesque village, which nestles in the bosom of the

surrounding mountains, and reminds one of a young bird in its nest. A rivulet, which sometimes steals around the obstacles to its course, sometimes bounds over them with headlong leap, at last finds its way to the valley beneath, and glides by the village in peace and beauty.[10]

Front Royal was about forty miles from the Manassas battleground and an extensive emergency hospital was hastily set up there for wounded Confederates. Belle worked long hours caring for them:

> My office was a very laborious one, and my duties were painful in the extreme; but then, as always, I allowed but one thought to keep possession of my mind—the thought that I was doing all a woman could do in her country's cause.[11]

But all her dedication and resolve were not enough to overcome the powerful horrors of a battlefield hospital. The smells, the wounds, the gangrene, and the suffering were too intense. Tears came easily; blood and death appalled her. The physical toil and the long hours exhausted her; she tired quickly. Belle grew ill from the overwork and nervous tension, and returned to her Martinsburg home for a long rest.[12]

At the Front Royal hospital Belle had heard some wounded soldiers discussing army intelligence operations—espionage, scouting, and carrying information—and the idea appealed to her. She was adventurous, daring, and unafraid. Her grandfather, Captain Glenn, had served as a scout. Her friend Turner Ashby was a scout for Stonewall Jackson, and she personally knew a young Confederate courier, Betty Duvall, a "lovely, fragile-looking girl, remarkable for the sweetness of her disposition."[13]

> A few days before the battle of Bull Run, a country market-cart stopped in the Confederate lines, at the door of General Bonham's tent. A peasant-girl alighted from the cart and begged for an immediate interview with the general. It was granted.
>
> "General Bonham, I believe?" said the young lady in tones which betrayed her superiority to the disguise she had assumed. Then, tearing down her long, black hair, she took from its folds a note, small, damp, and crumpled; it was by acting upon this informal dispatch that General Beauregard won the victory of Bull Run.

Miss D. had passed through the whole of the Federal army. I dare not now publish her name; but, if ever these pages meet her eye, she will not fail to recognize her own portrait, nor will she be displeased to find that her exiled countrywoman [Belle wrote this account in England] cherishes the remembrance of her intrepidity and devotion.[14]

Rose O'Neil Greenhow had written the dispatch. She was among the South's most notorious female espionage agents.

Belle felt certain that she could do what the daring Betty Duvall and Rose Greenhow had done. In the meantime, however, she would recover her health through relaxation, remaining in Martinsburg under the protective care of her mother and family.

In October 1861, Belle and her mother left to visit her father in the Confederate camp at Manassas. They stayed in a large house situated in the center of the camp, which was used as temporary quarters for wives, daughters, and friends of the soldiers. The children were left at home under the care of Grandmother Glenn and Eliza.[15]

That Belle's father was proud of his daughter's energetic devotion to the South is clearly revealed in her book. He himself had volunteered, despite his age, large family, many responsibilities, and the fact that no one would have expected him to fight. However, he decided that someone else could manage his store and farm while he served his country.[16] He was not surprised when Belle decided to dedicate herself to the cause of the Confederacy.

It was during this visit to Manassas that Belle officially became a courier. It is not known how she received the appointment, but her connections were numerous—her father was popular among the officers, and relatives at the camp must have included Mrs. Boyd's brother, Lieutenant James William Glenn. Family friend Turner Ashby, leader of Jackson's 7th Virginia Cavalry, was also at the camp and perhaps Glenn mentioned his niece's name and ambition to Ashby.[17]

Harry Gilmor, an officer in Company F of the same regiment with James Glenn, may have promoted the idea, out of admiration for Belle. In his 1866 book, *Four Years in the Saddle*, he praised the courage and devotion to the Confederacy of the "Southern girl whom I had known since the autumn of '61."[18]

In any event, Belle became a member of the Confederate Intelligence Service. "During this period I had frequently the honor of acting the part of courier to General Beauregard, General Jackson, and their subordinates."[19] She absorbed the mechanics of the trade like an eager child, learning many tactics from Turner Ashby, chief source of intelligence for Jackson and head of military scouts in the Shenandoah Valley.

A favorite ploy of Ashby's was to don civilian clothes and ride into Union camps, posing as a veterinarian. He would treat ailing horses, converse with riders, thus picking up important information. Other sources for Ashby's information were residents whose homes had been commandeered as quarters for Federal officers. They overheard confidential discussions and would bring intelligence to Ashby.[20] Belle carried much of this information to Jackson and Beauregard, often risking her life to do so. Her horse, Fleeter, was trained to kneel on command which enabled Belle to evade detection by Union patrols by making her less visible in the woods.[21]

In addition to espionage, Belle broadened her activities to include systematic pilfering of weapons—pistols, ammunition, and sabers—desperately needed by the poorly armed South. Medical supplies, especially quinine, were also a valued smuggling objective. In later years, a letter would reveal that Belle had been not only a spy, but that she had run the land blockade with much-needed quinine for malaria victims in Virginia.[22]

> I had been confiscating and concealing their pistols and swords on every possible occasion, and many an officer, looking about everywhere for his missing weapons, little dreamed who it was that had taken them, or that they had been smuggled away to the Confederate camp, and were actually in the hands of their enemies, to be used against themselves.[23]

Belle's activities brought her much publicity, which was both flattering and hazardous. If she were again apprehended by Union troops, it would not be for defending herself or her mother, but for treason against the Union.

The Quiet Winter of 1861

WINTER 1861—SPRING 1862

*Have no fear, gentlemen,
of the "cowardly rebels."*[1]

AS THE WEATHER GREW COLDER at Manassas, Belle and her mother returned to spend the winter in Martinsburg. The town was quiet in a military way, with the focus of battle having shifted to Fredericksburg and Chancellorsville. Martinsburg had returned to Confederate hands, under Colonel Turner Ashby's Seventh Virginia Cavalry.[2]

In the winter lull, life went on as usual, with parties, festivals, dances, music, and sleigh rides. Fun and laughter displaced the terror of war. Colonel Ashby became a Master Mason and joined Equality Lodge No. 136, becoming a lodge brother of Ben Boyd.[3]

One somewhat military incident did occur that quiet winter and it well illustrates Belle's audacity and ability to get away with anything.

Conventional young ladies of Martinsburg would not have dreamed of riding with two men, but this did not deter Belle. With two young officers, a cousin and a friend, she embarked upon an afternoon horseback ride. Her spirited, nervous mount shied and ran off with her, crossing into Federally controlled territory outside of town. Her companions began to follow, but hesitated, waiting to see if Belle could regain control.

Her horse spun and pranced by the Union pickets, who watched amused as she finally brought the tiring creature to rein. Angry and embarrassed, she nervously eyed the Federals and decided that the only way out was bluff and femininity. She rode up to the officers in command of the pickets.

> *Belle*: I beg your pardon—you must know that I have been taking a ride with some of my friends; my horse ran away with me, and has carried me within your lines. I am your captive, but I beg you will permit me to return.
>
> *Officer*: We are exceedingly proud of our beautiful captive, but of course we cannot think of detaining you. May we have the honor of escorting you beyond our lines and restoring you to the custody of your friends? I suppose there is no fear of those cowardly rebels taking us prisoners?
>
> *Belle*: I had scarcely hoped for such an honor. I thought you would probably have given me a pass; but since you are so kind as to offer your services in person, I cannot do otherwise than accept them. Have no fear, gentlemen, of the "cowardly rebels."[4]

"Cowardly rebels," indeed! Belle concealed her anger and started with the officers toward Confederate territory. Crossing the Federal boundary, they passed by some shrubbery from which emerged Belle's riding companions.

"Here are two prisoners that I have brought you," Belle cried to her friends. Turning to the Federals, she added, "Here are two of the 'cowardly rebels' whom you hoped there was no danger of meeting."

One of the dismayed Union soldiers queried, "And who, pray, is the lady?"

"Belle Boyd, at your service," she responded.

"Good God! The rebel spy!"

"So be it, since your journals have honored me with the title."[5]

The Union officers attempted no resistance as Belle and her companions escorted them to the Confederate headquarters in Martinsburg. There the officer in command detained them briefly while the Yankees bitterly reproached Belle for her treachery, but she felt they deserved some humiliation for their arrogance, and especially for the phrase "cowardly rebels"!

The Union officers were released within the hour and nothing further came of the incident, except for Belle and her companions gleefully relating their story again and again to their friends. Belle said of the incident: "I consoled myself that 'all was fair in love and war.' "[6]

The citizens of Martinsburg still anticipated a quick victory or a prompt reconciliation between North and South. Since hostilities had subsided during the winter months, they dared to hope for peace. But with the coming of spring, and no sign of reconciliation, they realized that the struggle would be long. It was with sad hearts that they watched Colonel Ashby and his cavalry leave town for other duties in the spring of 1862. The "Knight of the Valley" was a loved and trusted favorite in the Shenandoah Valley.[7]

> He united in himself all those qualifications which justly recommend their possessor to the love of the one sex and to the esteem of the other. At once tender and respectful, animated and handsome, he won without an effort the hearts of women. Brave and good humored, he combined simplicity with talents of the highest order. He entertained a strict sense of honor, and never forgot what was due to himself; and he was ever wont to forget an injury, and even to pardon an insult, upon the first overture of the offender. Such a man was sure to be among the first to draw his sword in the cause of independence.[8] Astride his white horse, he played games with the enemy on the fields of northern Virginia, but was shot down by enemy's bullets shortly before the engagement at Cross Keys in 1862.[9]

After the Battle of Bull Run President Lincoln placed General George B. McClellan in command of the forces around Washington. McClellan spent the next few months drilling his soldiers into a regular army, for when his fighting machine was perfected, he would march on Richmond. By the spring of 1862 the Confederates had a powerful army in the East, under two of the ablest commanders of the war, Generals Joseph E. Johnston and Robert E. Lee.[10]

Instead of attacking Richmond directly, McClellan decided to attack from the rear. Although the distance between the two capitals is barely a hundred miles by land, McClellan decided to send his army by sea—down the Potomac and up the James—and he became mired in the futile Peninsula Campaign. He was unable to take Richmond, nor were the Confederates strong enough to advance on Washington. Both sides dug in for a long war.[11]

A Restless Springtime

────────────────────────────────────

(1862)

Rare photo of Belle Boyd at age 19, found in the papers of Belle's 1944 biographer, Louis A. Sigaud. This is believed to be the first publication of this haunting image, by "Gardner, Washington, DC." Excerpt from the handwritten caption found in Sigaud's papers: ". . . photograph of Belle Boyd taken by order of Secretary of War Stanton during her imprisonment and not heretofore published . . . . found among the private papers of the Yankee spy, Pryce Lewis . . . [who was] an Old Capitol Prison guard when Stanton had the photograph taken." (Courtesy of the estate of Louis A. Sigaud.)

∬ CHAPTER SIX *∿*

No Place
to Hide

SPRING 1862

Manage to give it to me.
I am already a prisoner;
besides, free or in chains, I shall always
glory in the possession of the emblem.[1]

THE FEDERALS HAD DEFEATED General Jackson at Kernstown (near Winchester) and proceeded southward to Front Royal which they now occupied. The Stewarts, thinking that they would be both safer and of greater service if they were living in the capital of the Confederacy, decided to move to Richmond.[2]

Belle, too, made another move at this time. Martinsburg, at the northern border of Virginia, was in constant danger of reoccupation by Union forces. In the spring of 1862 Ben Boyd came home on sick leave, and as he reflected upon his daughter's safety, he decided to send her further south. Accordingly, Belle and Eliza left for Front Royal until Martinsburg should be once more secure.[3]

Grandmother Glenn was a widow and spent most of her time with her two daughters, Mary Boyd and Mrs. Stewart. She agreed to remain in Front Royal and look after the Stewarts's home, which was also a small hotel called the Strickler House (formerly known as Fishback's). The Stewarts had bought and managed the hotel upon leaving Washington. Their daughter Alice and Belle were left behind with their grandmother; the two girls were eighteen and could help in operating the hostelry. But, with the Federals occupying Front Royal, Belle again felt in jeopardy, having "jumped from the frying pan into the fire," as she put it.[4]

When I found that the Confederate forces were retreating so far down the Valley, and reflected that my father was with them, I became very anxious to return to my mother; and, as no tie of duty bound me to Front Royal, I resolved upon the attempt at all hazards.[5]

General Shields was the Federal commander in Front Royal. As he was quite fond of Belle, she had no difficulty in securing a travel pass from him. In a moment of protectiveness, he perhaps felt that Belle would be better off with her mother. Ironically, at that very time, the Provost Marshal (Shields's inferior) was issuing a contradictory order forbidding Belle to travel![6]

Belle and Eliza departed Front Royal, reaching Winchester without mishap. Here the Provost Marshal interfered because a suspicious person had denounced Belle as a spy. As Belle boarded the train, an officer who was taking some prisoners to Baltimore noticed her and suspected her identity.

"I am Captain Bannon. Is this Miss Belle Boyd?"

"Yes."

"I am the Assistant Provost and I regret to say orders have been issued for your detention. It is my duty to inform you that you cannot proceed until your case has been investigated. So you will, if you please, get out, as the train is on the point of starting."

Belle quickly produced the travel pass from Shields. "Sir, here is a pass which I beg you will examine. You will find that it authorizes my maid and me to pass on any road to Martinsburg."[7]

Captain Bannon was impressed and bewildered. If he detained her, he flouted General Shields's order; if he allowed her to proceed, he disobeyed the detention order of his immediate superior. And the train was about to leave! Bannon solved his dilemma by the time-honored method of passing the buck: "Well, I scarcely know how to act in your case. Orders have been issued for your arrest and yet you have a pass from the General allowing you to return home. However, I shall take the responsibility on my shoulders, convey you with [my] other prisoners to Baltimore; and hand you over to General Dix [the Union commandant]."[8]

Belle then played the role of submission as gracefully as she knew how. They had not proceeded far when she noticed an old friend and Southern sympathizer, Mr. M. of Baltimore, seated across the aisle.

At her invitation he sat beside her, and as they conversed, he whispered that he had a small Confederate flag.

Belle's eyes twinkled. "Manage to give it to me. I am already a prisoner; besides, free or in chains, I shall always glory in the possession of the emblem."

Mr. M. watched his opportunity and, when no one was looking, he quickly transferred the little flag from his vest pocket to Belle's hand. With a gesture of triumph she laughingly waved it over their heads as if she had won a great victory.[9]

Upon arriving in Baltimore, Bannon took Belle to the Eutaw House, one of the city's finest hotels, where she remained for about a week. She was treated as virtual royalty, receiving a stream of visitors, old friends, and Southern sympathizers. General Dix could find no reason to detain Belle and decided to release her, overriding the act of his field subordinate. She was returned to Martinsburg.[10]

In this hasty disposition of her case Belle was very fortunate; it is doubtful other Federal generals would have released her so readily. Many considered mere accusation, without proof of guilt, sufficient reason for prolonged imprisonment. However, General Dix opposed the arrest of civilians on suspicion only, explaining his position in a letter to General Mansfield several months later, stating that no person should be arrested on suspicion, nor confined to punishment, without clear evidence of guilt.[11]

Belle returned in mid-May to a Martinsburg that was once again in Federal possession. The Federals distrusted her more than ever. She was kept under constant scrutiny and forbidden to go beyond the limits of the town. With towns changing hands with unnerving frequency it was difficult to have a truly "safe" place to stay. Contrary to her daughter's logic, Belle's mother believed that Front Royal would be safer for Belle, so Mrs. Boyd appealed to the Provost for a travel pass. He probably was as anxious to get rid of Belle as she was to get away and Mrs. Boyd quickly secured a pass for their travel to Front Royal by way of Winchester. Once in Front Royal they hoped to get permission for Belle to go to Richmond.[12]

Upon arriving at Winchester, Belle and her mother were stopped. Front Royal's commander, General Shields, had prohibited all travel between there and Winchester. However, Belle had discovered that the Provost was gallant and susceptible and, after much persuasion by the two travelers, he relented and allowed them to proceed.

It was almost twilight when they arrived at the Shenandoah River, only to discover that the bridge had been destroyed. The one way across the river was a ferry boat that was monopolized by Union soldiers. Again the two travelers exercised their powers of persuasion. The captain allowed them to cross and provided for their transportation to Front Royal where they were turned over to General Shields.[13]

It was dark when they reached the Strickler House in Front Royal. They were tired, hungry, and dismayed to learn that the hotel had been taken over by the Federals and was now occupied by General Shields and his staff! Grandmother Glenn and Alice Stewart were now quartered on the hotel grounds in a small dwelling known today as the "Belle Boyd Cottage."[14]

Belle and her mother joined her grandmother and Alice at the cottage and, after dinner, Belle sent her card to General Shields. He called immediately to pay his respects, accompanied by an aide-de-camp, Captain Daniel Keily. A cordial evening was had by all, and not the least by Captain Keily, who became captivated by Belle (but more about that later).[15]

The following morning Belle sought a travel pass from General Shields to go to Richmond. The jolly Irishman received her good-naturedly, but refused the pass, assuring her that Jackson's army would be annihilated within a few days and she would then be free to leave Front Royal.[16] Forbidden to leave, Belle could only make the most of her situation. The Strickler House, as Shields's headquarters, was a hub of activity—on the main street, near the railroad station, with officers and soldiers everywhere. Such a situation was ideal for espionage.

At this time Belle ran across an old friend whom she had known in Martinsburg: David Hunter Strother of nearby Berkeley Springs, a famous artist and author known by his pen name "Porte Crayon." He was serving as a civilian map-maker with the Federal forces. That two young people from the same area elected opposite sides in the conflict was typical of northern Virginia, where loyalties were divided and much controversy existed. Strother's artistic eye found Belle "looking well and deporting herself in a very lady-like manner. I daresay she had been slandered by reports (in the press). She sported a bunch of buttons despoiled from General Shields and our officers and seemed ready to increase her trophies."[17]

Captain K
and a Midnight Ride

MAY 1862

*These are the days of war, not love,
and there are other ladies in the world
besides the rebel spy.*[1]

BELLE WAS NEAR HER eighteenth birthday and it was springtime.
General Shields's handsome young aide-de-camp, Captain Keily, did
not escape Belle's notice, nor did Belle escape his. Came the flowers,
and notes, and gifts, and romance was abloom.

Let us not forget, however, Belle's deeper romance with the
Southern cause, for Belle certainly did not forget it. She savored the
candy and the flowers, treasured the notes, and reported intelligence
from Keily's indiscreet remarks. Belle gives us a jolting reminder of her
adeptness at playing the games of love and war: "Let Capt. K. be
consoled; these are days of war, not love, and there are other ladies in
the world besides the rebel spy."[2]

From Captain K, Belle learned of a council meeting to be held in
the drawing room of the Strickler House on the evening of 14 or 15
May 1862. Attendees were to be General Shields, Captain K, and all of
Shields's officers. Belle was delighted with this information dropped by
Captain K and planned to take advantage of it. She knew well the floor
plan of the Strickler House, plus an opportune peculiarity of the old
hotel: immediately above the drawing room was a bedroom containing
a modest closet where a small hole had once been bored in the floor for
reasons lost to history.[3]

On the night of the meeting Belle hastened from the cottage to the hotel. Encountering no one, she stationed herself in the closet to await the meeting. Since Belle does not tell us precisely what happened, we can imagine what she perhaps experienced in the closet's cramped rectangle. . . .

The mustiness and mothballs of decades weighted her nose and the tails of shirts and coats rested intimately upon her neck and back. As her restlessness grew into irritation, a door opened in the drawing room below and ensuing laughter, scooting chairs, and paper rattling signalled the gathering of the council. To Belle's delight, she could not only clearly hear conversations, but could recognize the voices as well.

Shields's rumble dominated the session. There was much discussion and disagreement, even occasional fist thumping for emphasis. Belle's excitement was nearly uncontainable, being a silent party to first hand detail of planned moves, numbers, arms, and treachery. But Keily's gentle voice periodically reached Belle, quickening her heart and passion, taunting her with paradox, teaching how an unfaithful spouse must feel.

As midnight approached, Belle had experienced quite enough. Her knees hurt from the hardness of the bare oak floor; her shoulders ached; the clothing hanging above her seemed to be gradually descending to mummify her contorted form; her dress and hair were soaked with perspiration; and rancid cigar smoke (Shields's, no doubt) that had drifted up through the hole had assaulted her throat.

Returning to Belle's account, mercifully, the conference ended around one A.M. A grateful Belle awaited the last fading clatter after the door closed downstairs and then crawled from her post. Slipping from the Strickler House, she crossed the courtyard, relishing the sudden coolness of the night air upon her damp person, and returned to her room in the cottage. She hurriedly enciphered a note telling all that she had overheard.[4]

Belle's next problem was to get the news to Ashby. If she aroused a servant to carry her note it would cause a disturbance and might create suspicion. She must go herself; there was no other way! Slipping out to the stables, she saddled her horse and led him quietly into the bright moonlight, some distance away from the house. She then mounted and rode quickly toward Strasburg, some fifteen miles westward, where she knew Turner Ashby was quartered.[5] (Ashby was near Strasburg to harass, by repeated raids, Federal forces under General Nathaniel Banks.[6]) Belle had wisely taken with her several travel passes acquired from paroled Confederate soldiers returning south.

> They [false passes] proved invaluable; for I was twice brought to a standstill by the challenge of the Federal sentries, and who would inevitably have put a period to my adventurous career had they not been beguiled by my false passport.[7]

Belle does not tell us whether the sentries questioned why an eighteen-year-old girl was riding at two A.M. in wartime!

Once clear of sentries, she dashed on toward Strasburg, across the fields, over rail fences, and through the thick woods. After a furious ride she reached Strasburg's outskirts and the home where she understood Colonel Ashby was spending the night.

All was still and dark; the din of spring peepers filled the cool night air. Belle reined in her horse with a clatter, bounded to the door, and pounded with such vehemence that the entire house resounded. There was no answer. Belle repeated her pounding, and finally an upstairs window was raised.

"Who is there?"

"It is I," cried Belle.

"But who are you? What is your name?"

"Belle Boyd. I have important intelligence to communicate to Colonel Ashby. Is he here?"

"No; but wait a minute; I will come down."

Soon the door opened and a man whom Belle called "Mr. M" drew her inside the entrance hall. "My dear, where did you come from? How on earth did you get here?"

"Oh, I forced the sentries and here I am; but I have no time to tell you the how, and the why, and the wherefore. I must see Colonel Ashby without the loss of a minute; tell me where he is to be found."[8]

In his effort to protect Ashby, Mr. M misinformed Belle as to the whereabouts of the Colonel, telling her that Ashby was a quarter of a mile farther up the road. Belle was remounting her horse when a door was thrown open, revealing Colonel Ashby. "Good God! Miss Belle, is this you? Where did you come from? Have you dropped from the clouds? Or am I dreaming?"[9]

Brushing aside Ashby's astonishment, Belle excitedly narrated all she had overheard in the closet, her words pouring forth in haste and excitement. She handed him the note, bade him goodnight, and rode off as abruptly as she had appeared.

Belle felt happy on the return trip, pleased in the knowledge of a mission accomplished. But she could not linger on the route home to enjoy the beauty of the night; her absence might be discovered.

> I arrived safely at my aunt's house, after a two hours' ride, in the course of which I "ran the blockade" of a sleeping sentry, who awoke to the sound of my horses hoofs just in time to see me disappear round an abrupt turning, which shielded me from the bullet he was about to send me.[10]

Quietly riding into the stable, she administered a quick rubdown to her exhausted mount and crept into the cottage. The morning sunrise saw her to bed, where she slept soundly and at peace, knowing that her message would reach Jackson.

Like all good spies, Belle never revealed to anyone what she heard, other than to those having a need to know. However, we can conjecture what she heard in that closet on that May night from other sources: evidently, Belle overheard a scheme to lay a trap for "poor old Jackson and his demoralized army." If Stonewall were to act promptly on what Belle was overhearing, he could avoid capture, and actions that Jackson would take over the next few days indicate that he did just that.[11]

And what of poor Captain K, the young knight so skillfully used by the enemy queen? Wounded at the Battle of Port Republic in June, he was taken to Front Royal to recover at Oakley, Colonel Ashby's home. There Belle Boyd, doubtless remembering the flowers and love notes, and perhaps fishing for further information, visited him.[12]

Belle's visits to see the Union officer shocked the citizens of Front Royal who did not know of their special relationship. They would, perhaps, have been even more shocked had they realized that Belle's visits were a quixotic amalgam of love, human kindness toward the enemy, and espionage!

Captain K recovered, was cited for bravery,[13] and eventually promoted to Brigadier General.[14]

PART THREE

The Heroine
of Front Royal

(1862)

Among the best-known photos of Belle Boyd (age 19) taken by Gardner of Washington DC, by order of Secretary of War Stanton upon her release from the Old Capitol Prison, December, 1863. The picture was found among the papers of Pryce Lewis. (Courtesy of Laura Virginia Hale and the Warren Rifles Confederate Museum, both Front Royal VA.)

Lieutenant
H

MAY 1862

. . . you profess to be a great friend of mine.
Prove it by assisting me out of this dilemma . . .[1]

BELLE, HER GRANDMOTHER GLENN, and Alice Stewart remained in the little cottage behind the Strickler House in Front Royal. Mrs. Boyd had returned to Martinsburg to be with the younger children. Front Royal remained under Union control. General Shields departed to trap Jackson, or so he hoped, leaving behind an occupation army of about 1,000—one squadron of cavalry, one field battery, and the First Maryland Regiment of Infantry under Colonel Kenley. Tents were pitched in the courthouse yard and the town was all activity and confusion. Major Tyndale assumed control as Provost Marshal.[2]

One of Belle's contemporaries, Lucy Buck, lived in a beautiful mansion, Bel Air, just outside of town. Lucy was older than Belle and "one of her chief critics."[3] A few days after Belle's eighteenth birthday, the Federals took possession of Bel Air. Lucy describes the occasion:

> *May 14, 1862.* An ever memorable day to the inhabitants of Bel Air. . . . I went downstairs and, observing an unusual stir at the door, I stepped on the porch to learn the cause. General Kimball's brigade would be in immediately to quarter in the meadows in front of the house. . . . We soon heard notes from the band and, looking toward the depot, saw the head of the column advancing into the field. On they came—

a dark mass of human beings winding through the meadows like a great black serpent until the whole 4,000 were in the two fields. They were a sorry looking sight, wet and muddy, their dripping banners clinging to the staff. Next came the wagon trains and the artillery . . . Father's beautiful stone fence had to be leveled to afford them egress—they turned their horses into the clover field.[4]

The officers then established their headquarters in the west wing of Bel Air. The soldiers of the brigade burned the rail fences around a fifty-acre wheat field as well as the greater part of the plank fencing, locust posts and oak planks surrounding the timothy meadow of twenty-eight acres adjoining the town. They also burned one-third of the rail fence from a field of thirty-five acres of clover.[5]

Belle and Alice, restless from inactivity, decided to take advantage of the blossoming springtime around them and visit friends in Winchester. On 20 May they applied to Major Tyndale for a pass. At first he declined but at the girls' persistence, he promised to issue one the following morning.[6]

Next morning, 21 May, the girls arose early and, accompanied by Eliza, prepared to leave. Their carriage was at the door, but no pass arrived. Major Tyndale, they were informed, had "gone out on scout" and would not return until late that night. Disappointed and angry, they were trying to decide what to do when Belle recognized a young Yankee officer she called "Lieutenant H."

Lieutenant H announced that he was leaving for Winchester. How opportune! Knowing that Union pickets were stationed along the route, and that without a pass they would be harassed or even arrested, the girls asked if they might accompany him. He balked, but Belle persisted, "Now, Lieutenant H, I know that you have permission to go to Winchester, and you profess to be a great friend of mine: prove it by assisting me out of this dilemma, and pass us through the pickets."[7] Perhaps considering the consequences, Lieutenant H hesitated again, but then consented. He helped the girls into the carriage.

Lucy Buck had arisen early that morning to write a letter and Belle was to slip it through the Union lines. Upon arriving at the Strickler House, Lucy was stunned to find Belle seated in a carriage with the Yankee officer. While Lucy disapproved of Belle's unconventional behavior, she had been perfectly willing to let Belle run the risk of delivering her letter within the enemy lines. However, she was so appalled that Belle would be brazen enough to ride to Winchester escorted by a Yankee officer that she decided not to entrust the letter to her. Lucy departed in a huff, and Belle, Alice, Eliza, and Lieutenant H headed northward into the fine spring morning.[8]

Following a pleasant and uneventful trip, they arrived in Winchester, where the girls stayed overnight with friends, planning to return to Front Royal the next day when Lieutenant H had completed his business.[9]

Early the next morning a well-dressed gentleman of high social position (Belle does not identify him)[10] came to the house and handed Belle two packages of letters. He gave definite instructions regarding them, handing her one package and saying that it was of great importance. He then handed her the other package, saying that it was a comparative trifle. Finally he handed over a little note, a most crucial document that had to safely reach General Jackson or his equal. "Do you understand?" the gentleman asked Belle. "I do, and will obey your orders promptly and implicitly."[11]

An unnoticed servant who had viewed this exchange faded from the room, quietly slipped out of the house, and reported what he had seen. This occasioned a telegram to Major Tyndale in Front Royal. Already angry with Belle for her unapproved trip to Winchester, Tyndale grew livid. He immediately contacted George H. Beal, officer-in-charge in Winchester, ordering Belle's arrest.[12]

Belle concealed the more important package of letters in Eliza's clothing because blacks were generally beyond suspicion. She wrote "Kindness of Lieutenant H" upon the other bundle of letters and placed them in a small basket on her arm. The small note rested carelessly in her hand as if unimportant.[13]

Although unaware of Tyndale's order to arrest her, Belle knew perfectly well that traveling without a pass was very dangerous, and that she, Eliza, and Alice were out on a limb. And now, carrying confidential material added further to their jeopardy. With a need to have the right people on her side immediately, she forwarded a beautiful bouquet to Lieutenant Colonel James A. Fillebrown, Winchester's Provost Marshal, along with a request for a pass to Front Royal. The easily-flattered Fillebrown took the bait, forwarded the pass, and enclosed a note thanking Belle for "so sweet a compliment."[14]

Belle, Alice, and Eliza rejoined Lieutenant H, who had finished his errands, and began their return journey to Front Royal. Belle had just begun to congratulate herself on the success of their trip when Federal detectives halted them at the picket lines outside Winchester. Belle was arrested on suspicion of carrying letters to Confederate officers. The travelers were taken to Colonel Beal's headquarters. Alice was frightened, Lieutenant H was dismayed, Eliza was puzzled, but Belle was unshaken.

"Have you any illegal letters?" demanded Beal. Knowing that denying the charge would provoke a search of her clothing and baggage, Belle bluffed. She drew from her basket the trifling bundle of letters and handed it to the Colonel. Beal spotted the note, "Kindness of Lieutenant H" on the bundle, and became instantly suspicious of the young officer.

"What! What is this? Kindness of Lieutenant H! What does this mean? Is this all you have?"

"Look for yourself—as for this scribbling on the letter, it means nothing; it was a thoughtless act of mine. I assure you Lieutenant H knew nothing about the letter or that it was in my possession."[15]

Then Beal turned his attention to the note in Belle's hand. "What is this you have in your hand?"

"What—this little scrap of paper? You can have it if you wish. It is nothing." She approached the Colonel with the seeming intention of placing it in his hand. The bluff succeeded as Beal's wrath was diverted from the guilty to the guiltless. He was so angry with Lieutenant H that he ignored Belle and the precious note, dismissing the girls but ordering Lieutenant H kept under surveillance. Belle noted, "Had it not been for the curious manner in which Lieutenant H was involved in the affair, and in which that unoffending officer was so unjustly treated, very much to my regret, I should not have escaped so easily."[16]

Lieutenant H was subsequently investigated, court-martialled, and dismissed from the service. Belle regretted involving him, but she had succeeded, once again, in talking her way out of serious difficulty.[17] (Lieutenant H was probably Lieutenant Abram H. Hasbrouck of the 5th New York Cavalry. He was stationed in Front Royal at the time.[18])

The girls were allowed to continue their journey to Front Royal, a move that the North would regret the very next day, for on that day the Battle of Front Royal would occur, and Belle's actions would prove disastrous to the Union forces.

The Battle
of Front Royal

23-24 MAY 1862

I looked for Belle Boyd and I found her. . . .
As I stooped from my saddle she pinned a crimson rose
to my uniform, bidding me remember that it was blood red
and that it was her "colors.¹"

BELLE WAS HAPPY to return to Front Royal after the incident with Lieutenant H and Colonel Beal. She loved Front Royal as much as she did Martinsburg and her sentiments echoed those of another Civil War veteran, Richard Taylor, a brigade leader under Stonewall Jackson who noted:

> The situation of [Front Royal] is surprisingly beautiful. It lies near the east bank of the Shenandoah, which just below unites all its waters [North Fork and South Fork], and looks directly on the northern peaks of Massanutten [mountain range]. The Blue Ridge, with Manassas Gap, through which passes the railway, overhangs it on the East; distant Allegheny [mountain range] bounds the horizon to the West; and down the Shenandoah the eye ranges over a fertile, well-farmed country. Two bridges spanned the river, a wagon bridge above, a railroad bridge some yards lower. A good pike led to Winchester, twenty miles. . . .²

Belle had developed a personal problem with a particular Yankee in Front Royal, Mr. A. W. Clark, a correspondent for the *New York Herald* who, according to Belle, was "by no means a gentleman." He resided at the Strickler House and Belle saw him daily as she could not reach the street from her cottage without crossing the courtyard and passing through the hallway of the Strickler House. Clark showed interest in Belle but she resisted his advances. He persevered to such an extent that she and Alice were forced, more than once, to bolt the door of their sitting-room against him. He was stung by these rebuffs and very shortly would be stung far more severely by Belle's actions.[3]

The day following her return from Winchester, Belle acquired some crucial news—yet another Union plan was afoot to disable Stonewall Jackson, who was heading northward through the valley. This time, five different forces were to combine against him: General Banks in Strasburg with 4,000 men, the small force at Winchester, General Julius White's troops at Harpers Ferry, Generals Shields and Geary near Front Royal, and General Fremont in the west just beyond the Shenandoah Valley.[4]

Belle realized that the way out for Jackson was for him to attack Front Royal before these forces could unite. She determined to carry this intelligence to Jackson, but how to reach him? As she pondered this, a servant rushed in. "Oh, Miss Belle, I t'inks de revels am a-comin', for de Yankees are a-makin' orful fuss in de street."[5]

Belle rushed to the door. The streets were thronged with Union soldiers, hurrying in every direction in great confusion. Running into the street, she sought a friendly Federal officer and queried him. He explained that scouts had reported Confederates approaching the town in force, under Generals Jackson and Ewell. There was chaos because no one had any idea that Jackson was so close—he was believed to be fifty miles to the southwest near Harrisonburg on the other side of the massive Massanutten Mountain ridge. Instead of the Federals surprising Jackson, just the opposite was happening— except that Jackson did not yet know of his golden opportunity to attack and drive the disorderly Union troops from Front Royal![6]

"Well, with Jackson so close, what are you going to do?" Belle asked the officer.

"Now we are endeavoring to get the ordnance and the quarter- master's stores out of their [Jackson's] reach."

"But what will you do with the stores in the large depot?" Belle continued.

"Burn them, of course."

"But suppose the rebels come upon you too quickly?"

"Then we will fight as long as we can by any possibility—show a front, and in the event of defeat make good our retreat upon Winchester, burning the [wagon and railroad] bridges as soon as we cross them, and finally effect a junction with General Bank's force."[7]

That was all Belle needed to hear. She rushed back to the Strickler House. When racing up the stairs, she ran headlong into Mr. Clark, the reporter. "Great Heavens! What is the matter?" exclaimed Clark.

"Nothing to speak of—only the rebels are coming and you had best prepare yourself for a visit to Libby Prison [in Richmond]!"[8]

Clark looked stunned and without a word turned and ran back up the stairs toward his room. Belle continued up the stairs behind him, pausing to grab a pair of field glasses on her way to the balcony. Her route took her by Clark's open door and she saw that he was furiously packing his bags and destroying some papers. Noting his door key on the outside, the temptation was too strong to resist! She quietly closed the door, turned the key with a decisive click, and went on her way, cackling gleefully at her revenge against this Yankee pest!

From the balcony Belle saw through her field glasses the advance guard of the Confederates, about three-quarters of a mile away, marching rapidly toward the town. Adding to her anxiety was the knowledge that her father, a member of the Stonewall Jackson Brigade, was among them! She, and only she, knew that the rebels must strike *right now*, while Shields's troops were in chaos and before Union reinforcements could arrive. As the Federal officer had just told her, if the rebels arrived too quickly, Union forces could only show a front and then retreat. She must reach Stonewall immediately.

Out on the street Belle spoke to several men who were ardent Southern loyalists, at least in their talk; now was the time for them to prove it. Would one of them take a note to Jackson? Only hemming and hawing met her request, and with disdain for their cowardice, she ran down the street. No time could be lost! Edging her way through the Union soldiers, past the heavy guns and equipment, she reached the outskirts of town. Continuing through the fields and scattered woods, she ran to meet the approaching Confederate troops, who were still beyond direct view of the town at street level.

The Federals had placed their artillery on a hill commanding the road by which the Confederates advanced. As the Confederates came into sight and the crossfire began, Belle was caught in the middle, with bullets flying thick and fast about her, striking the ground so near that dust was thrown in her eyes. Her dark blue dress with its little fancy white apron and her white sunbonnet rendered the valiant messenger very conspicuous. The contrasting colors in the midday sun made her an excellent target!

> Upon this occasion my life was spared by what seemed to me then, and seems still, little short of a miracle; for besides the numerous bullets that whistled by my ears, several actually pierced different parts of my clothing, but not one reached my body. . . . Federal and Confederate . . . shot and shell flew whistling and hissing over my head.[9]

At length a Federal shell struck the ground within twenty yards and Belle quickly threw herself on the ground. The explosion an instant later sent fragments flying all around her. Feeling as though providence had spared her life, she scrambled to her feet and continued to run toward the Confederates.

> I shall never run again as I ran on that, to me memorable day. Hope, fear, the love of life, and the determination to serve my country to the last, conspired to fill my heart with more than feminine courage, and to lend preternatural strength and swiftness to my limbs. I often marvel, and even shudder, when I reflect how I cleared the fields, and bounded over the fences with the agility of a deer.[10]

At last reaching the Southern advance guard, she waved her sunbonnet toward Front Royal as a signal to attack the town. Loud cheers rang out in reply and the soldiers began to rush forward. An awful thought suddenly struck her. She could not yet see the main body of the Confederate troops, as they were hidden from view by a slight elevation; what if the Southern force were too few in number and too weak to defeat the Federals? Her heart almost ceased to beat as she realized that she might have sent those gallant men to their deaths. Overcome by fatigue and a need for divine guidance, she sank upon her knees and prayed. Then,

> I felt as if my supplication was answered, and that I was inspired with fresh spirits and a new life. Not only despair,

but fear also forsook me; and I had again no thought but how
to fulfill the mission I had already pursued so far.[11]

As the rebels charged Front Royal, Belle arose and ran forward
again, seeking General Jackson. He had been at the rear of his force,
and as he rode to the fore, he joined his aide Henry Kyd Douglas on a
hilltop overlooking the town. It was Douglas who spotted the girl in the
white sunbonnet running toward them. In amazement, his mouth fell
open—he at once recognized Belle and reflected that "she was just the
girl to dare to do this thing."

Douglas rode toward Belle and she in turn recognized him. When
they met he seized her, demanding to know why in God's name she
was there! As the breathless girl became articulate, she gasped out her
news and urged him to hasten the entire force onward, to capture the
wagon and railroad bridges before they could be burned. Douglas
raised his cap, wheeled, and galloped away furiously to report to
Jackson. Belle kissed her hand to him.[12]

General Richard Taylor, commander of Jackson's advance units,
witnessed the encounter:

> . . . there rushed out of the wood to meet us a young, rather
> well-looking woman. . . . Breathless with speed and agitation,
> some time elapsed before she found her voice. Then, with
> much volubility, she said we were near Front Royal, beyond
> the wood; that the town was filled with Federals whose camp
> was on the west side of the [Shenandoah] river, where they
> had guns in position to cover the wagon bridge, but none
> bearing on the railway bridge below the former; that they
> believed Jackson to be west of Massanutten, near Harrison-
> burg; that General Banks, the Federal commander, was at
> Winchester, twenty miles northwest of Front Royal, where
> he was slowly concentrating his widely scattered forces to
> meet Jackson's advance, which was expected some days
> later. All this she told with the precision of a staff officer
> making a report, and it was true to the letter. . . .
>
> Convinced of the correctness of the woman's state-
> ments, I hurried forward at "a double" hoping to surprise the
> enemy's idlers in the town or swarm over the wagon bridge
> with them and secure it. Doubtless this was rash, but I felt

immensely "cocky" about my brigade, and believed that it would prove more [than] equal to any demand.[13]

The bugle notes, and yells, and whinnying of spurred horses in the clouds of dust told Belle that Jackson had indeed ordered a full charge. As the cavalry flew past her, Jackson rode up, his face wreathed in sweat, dirt, and smiles. He thanked Belle and offered her a horse and an escort for a safe return to town. But realizing that all men and mounts were needed in the attack, Belle declined and Jackson hastened after his troops.[14]

Belle returned home by the same route. A few minutes later Henry Kyd Douglas saw a flash of white at the edge of the village— Belle was waving her sunbonnet. She then disappeared among the houses of Front Royal.

> It took very little time to get into Front Royal and clean it out. The pursuit of the retreating Federals was kept up, with cavalry and infantry following as quickly as possible. While this was being done I looked for Belle Boyd and found her standing on the pavement in front of a hotel, talking with some few Federal officers (prisoners) and some of her acquaintances in our army. Her cheeks were rosy with excitement and recent exercise and her eyes were all aflame. When I rode up to speak to her she received me with much surprised cordiality, and, as I stooped from my saddle she pinned a rose to my uniform, bidding me remember that it was blood-red and that it was her "colors."[15]

Thanks to Belle's courageous run, the Confederates gained a complete victory at Front Royal. Although the depot building was burning and the bridges had been fired, Jackson's cavalry reached them in time to douse the flames and save them from destruction. Many Confederates burned their hands severely while tossing flaming brands into the river and General Taylor's horse and clothing were badly scorched.[16]

> May 23, 1862.

Miss Belle Boyd,

> I thank you, for myself and for the army, for the immense service that you rendered your country today.

> Hastily I am your friend,
> T. J. Jackson C.S.A.

Completely unprepared for Stonewall's note, Belle was deeply touched. It was written at the Richard house just beyond Front Royal and was delivered to Belle by a courier. "I am free to confess, I value it far beyond anything I possess in the world," Belle later wrote.[17]

This note has been the focus of much interest, not only because of the great honor it conveys to Belle from Jackson, but also because it has never been found. Louis Sigaud: "It is known that many of [Belle's] papers were destroyed in a fire . . . that others, turned over by her to her daughter . . . have been missing . . . [but] lack of confirmation is not affirmative proof that they were not [written]. Until Belle Boyd's present remarkable record of accuracy can be successfully impeached, it is reasonable to assume that on this, as on other matters, she told the truth."[18]

Belle had indeed been the heroine of the day at Front Royal. Word of her feat spread through the town and soon throughout the Shenandoah Valley. Newspapers south and north reported the daring act of this youthful rebel, although not all of the reports praised her.[19]

The Northern press was severely critical and Belle blamed this squarely upon Mr. Clark of the *New York Herald*. She certainly had cause for her belief, for after she had locked him in his room, he had escaped through a window, but this took time and the delay caused his capture. They saw each other as he was led down the street with other prisoners. He cried out, "I'll make you rue this! It's your doing that I am a prisoner here!"[20]

Because Clark was an "innocent journalist," General Jackson had him released several hours after his capture. But as the not-so-innocent journalist departed Front Royal, he severed the ferry line across the Shenandoah. He was later to carry dispatches for the Union and to be cited for his valuable service as a volunteer aide![21]

The Confederates, following up their victory, crossed the river and pushed on toward Winchester. General Banks hurriedly left Strasburg, rushed through Winchester and Martinsburg, and finally retreated across the Potomac at Williamsport, Maryland. As Banks passed down the main street of Martinsburg, some children were standing on the sidewalk observing the retreat. Belle's little sister Mary was in the group. Recognizing General Banks's aide-de-camp, she approached him. "Captain, how long are you going to stay here?"

"Until Gabriel blows his horn."

"Ah, Captain, if you were to hear Jackson's horn just outside the town, you would not wait for Gabriel's."[22]

During the battle, while Colonel Fillebrown (the officer in Winchester whom Belle had flattered into giving her a pass to Front Royal) was preparing to join the retreat from the city, a gentleman stepped into Fillebrown's office. "Colonel, how on earth did you get into such a trap? Did you know nothing of the advance of the Confederates?"

Fillebrown, pointing to the flowers Belle had sent a few days before, answered wryly, "That bouquet did all the mischief; the donor of that gift is responsible for all the misfortune."[23]

The Rebel
Spy at Bay

(1862)

This photo of Belle Boyd, taken in her 40s, was reproduced in Curtis Carroll Davis's edition of Belle Boyd in Camp and Prison. To quote his caption: "Belle Boyd in stage costume, reciting 'The Perils of a Spy.' A rare undated likeness by Morris Photographers, 16 Sixth Street, Pittsburgh, Pa., personally autographed." (Photo courtesy of Laura Virginia Hale and the Warren Rifles Confederate Museum, both Front Royal VA; caption courtesy of C. C. Davis.)

CHAPTER TEN

He Ain't
No Secesh!

24 MAY—29 JULY 1862

. . . he ain't no secesh.
Can't fool Betsy dat way.
Dat man's a spy . . . please God he am![1]

AFTER THE BATTLE OF Front Royal the rebel wounded were brought into town and Belle briefly resumed her role as nurse. To her great joy, her father came safely from the battle, with but a very slight leg wound; after medical treatment he rejoined his regiment.[2]

During this interval, while the Confederates possessed the town, a Mrs. Annie Jones was taken into custody and confined in the Strickler House. She claimed to be the wife of a soldier from the Michigan cavalry. Sympathetically, Belle furnished her with clothing and comforted her. But then Union maneuvers forced Jackson to abandon Front Royal and withdraw up the valley to avoid being surrounded. This left the town open for Federal reoccupation which happened promptly. Annie Jones was freed and proceeded to demonstrate her ingratitude. She reported Belle to General Kimball as a "most dangerous rebel, and a malignant enemy of the Federal Government."[3]

General Kimball placed Belle under arrest, stationing sentries around the cottage. However, Belle was a double-edged problem. If they held her, they had to dedicate men to her constant surveillance, or imprison her outright. If they released her, she would certainly resume forwarding intelligence to the Confederates.

As it happened, within a few hours of her arrest, General Shields arrived. Knowing full well that Shields was the senior of General Kimball, Belle approached Shields with a smile and a helpless look. The ploy worked—he released her immediately. Belle thanked him and she was free again—at least until she would once more flutter too close to the flame in the not-too-distant future.

Meanwhile, General Banks had returned and encamped close to the town, making his headquarters at the Strickler House. Realizing her personal danger in Front Royal, Belle wanted to travel farther south and approached General Banks for permission.

"Where do you wish to go?" queried Banks.

"To Louisiana, where my aunt resides."

"But what will Virginia do without you?" he grinned.

"What do you mean, General?"

"We always miss our bravest and most illustrious, and how can your native state do without you?" Belle thanked him for the compliment, conversing pleasantly about her part in his recent defeat! He was courteous and amiable, but did not yield the requested passport. Although accustomed to getting her own way, she accepted his refusal, concealing her disappointment.[4]

June and July passed quietly. Front Royal was again evacuated by Federal troops, with only the 3rd Delaware Infantry remaining. Two officers who remained behind, Provost Marshal Major Arthur Maginnis and his assistant, Lieutenant Preston, were kind and respected by the townspeople.[5]

Major Maginnis came to know Belle and developed a fondness for her. After the war he would tell stories to his young daughter and stories about Belle became her favorites. The Major described her as "a very young, very fearless, and very foolish girl." But to his daughter, the last adjective was wrong, "I thought of her as beautiful, riding on a spirited horse to serve her country."[6]

On a day in late July of 1862, Belle observed two men, dressed as Confederate soldiers, standing by a tent near her cottage. It was at this tent that all passports to the South were processed. Told that the soldiers were paroled prisoners heading south, she invited them to dinner and had her Grandmother Glenn secure permission from Major Maginnis.[7]

Belle extended the invitation in person to one of the men who accepted gladly, but pointed out that he must leave soon after dinner as he had only a limited time to get beyond the Federal lines. This suggested an idea to Belle and she impulsively queried, "Won't you take a letter from me to General Jackson?" He readily agreed and she hastened toward her room to pen the note. But as she passed the kitchen door, a servant stopped her.

"Miss Belle! Who's dat man yose-a-talkin' to?"

"I know no more about him than that he is a paroled rebel soldier, going South."

"Miss Belle, dat man ain't no rebel. I seen him 'mong de Yankees in de street. If he is got secesh clothes on, he ain't no secesh. Can't fool Betsy dat way. Dat man's a spy—dat man's a spy. Please God he am!"[8]

Unconvinced, Belle brushed the warning aside. She continued to her room and wrote the letter to Jackson, giving information about the status and maneuvers of the Federal army near Front Royal.

As soon as dinner was finished, Belle took the soldier aside and entrusted the letter to him. "Will you promise me faithfully, upon the honor of a soldier, to take the utmost care of this, and deliver it safely to General Jackson? They tell me you are a spy, but I don't believe it." The soldier appeared perplexed, denied the accusation, and swore that he would deliver the message "with fidelity and dispatch."[9]

Later that evening a Federal officer advised Belle that the soldier was indeed a Federal spy, a Secret Service agent on his way to the Confederate lines. Belle broke out in a tingly sweat. What had she done? Her mind darted from one alternative to another. She finally decided to notify her old friend Major Harry Gilmor of the Confederate cavalry, describing the man, the circumstances of his journey south, and how she had erred in giving him information intended for Jackson.[10]

Belle sent the message by the "underground railroad." She concealed the letter in an enormous silver pocket watch from which the works had been removed and gave it to a black man-servant who was unlikely to be stopped. Blacks were often used as couriers since Northern forces naively believed that blacks were on *their* side! If anyone were to ask him the time of day, he would say, in all honesty, that his watch didn't work.

The message reached Gilmor and he replied via the same messenger: no man of that description had been seen there; he must have gone by another route. Belle was puzzled, but she soon learned the truth: the soldier's real name was C. W. D. Smitley, chief of scouts of the Cavalry of Western Virginia.[11] Indeed he was a Union spy, who had been sent to Front Royal specifically to entrap Belle, and he had succeeded admirably. She had found him warm and charming and even fancied herself in love with him!

After dining with Belle, Smitley had made his way straight to General Franz Sigel, commander of a Union corps in the valley. Sigel glanced at Belle's note to Jackson and immediately contacted Secretary of War Stanton in Washington.[12]

After Belle learned that Smitley was a spy, she endured agony. How could she have been so susceptible, so immature, so stupid? She could neither eat nor sleep; she became ill-tempered and abrupt. Belle knew that she was in great trouble this time—that she would not be able to bluff her way out. She must face the consequences. What would her punishment be? Belle pondered the warnings, given her several times before, that further misconduct would be followed by severe punishment. The intercepted letter was clear proof that she was sending information to Jackson.

Belle nervously decided to flee to Richmond and applied for a travel pass. An officer promised that a pass would be forthcoming (the Federals in Front Royal were willing enough to have her leave, just to get rid of this thorn in their side). It was on a Tuesday that she was promised a pass; Belle and Eliza would leave for Richmond on Thursday. But fate ordained otherwise.[13]

CHAPTER ELEVEN

A Prisoner

30-31 July 1862

*Melodrama always attended Belle
even when she did not create it.*[1]

EARLY ON THE MORNING of 30 July 1862 after breakfast, Belle stood on
the balcony of the cottage apprehensively watching the activities
below. The day was warm and the sunlight brilliant on the crowded
street. She observed several Union soldiers remove a carriage from
the coach house, hitch horses to it, and drive it to the door of Union
headquarters. With the uneasy feeling that the carriage might be for
her, she watched as the soldiers waited about the coach, killing time.

A servant came to the balcony. "Miss Belle, de Provo' wishes to
see you in de drawing room, and dere's two oder men wid him."[2] Belle
slowly descended the stairs, a terrible heartbeat in her chest. As she
entered the drawing room Major Maginnis greeted her nervously.
With him were two other men, Major Francis T. Sherman, and a
stranger—a stranger who looked so vile, coarse, suspicious, and
repulsive, that Belle fearfully appraised him in an instant as a creature
of cowardice, ferocity, and cunning.

"The Secretary of War has ordered you to prison in Washington," Major Sherman said. "This is Detective Cridge of the Secret
Service, and he will escort you to the capital."[3] Cridge smugly produced a confirming document:

War Department,
July 30, 1862.

Sirs: You will proceed immediately to Front Royal, Virginia, and arrest, if found there, Miss Belle Boyd, and bring her at once to Washington.

I am respectfully,
Your obedient servant,
E. M. Stanton.[4]

Prison! Belle was absolutely stunned! She had feared this, but hoped for a nasty reprimand instead. Why should her actions come to the personal attention of the Secretary of War? With a malicious glower, Cridge announced that he must examine her belongings. But there were papers he must not see! Belle humbly asked if she and her maid might go upstairs ahead of the visitors and make her room presentable. Cridge did not answer and Belle took the silence for consent. Eliza hurried upstairs with Belle close behind.

But the detective followed at her heels. Belle turned abruptly to him. "Sir, will you not wait until I see if my room is in a suitable condition for you to enter?"

"No, yer don't; I'm a-goin' wit yer. Yer got some papers yer want to get rid on."[5]

Brushing past her, Cridge barged into her room. He pawed through her clothes (upper garments and underwear), turning them inside out, littering the floor with them. He spotted her desk and began to search it, but Eliza had earlier anticipated his effort to find something and had cleared the desk of the most damaging documents, burning them in the kitchen. Cridge confiscated some papers that remained and helped himself to a handsome pistol that had been given to Belle on Independence Day, 1861, by a Federal officer who admired her defense of her mother when their home in Martinsburg was invaded.[6]

Not content with the papers he found, the detective also took some of Mr. Stewart's papers which had been left with Belle for safekeeping during his absence from Front Royal. Cridge then demanded that Belle be prepared to leave within the hour. Could Eliza accompany her? asked Belle, but Cridge refused. With the help of

Grandmother Glenn and Alice, the solitary trunk she was permitted to take was soon packed.

Belle returned to the drawing room and announced firmly, "I'm ready." Alice and Belle's grandmother wept, and Eliza passionately begged to accompany Belle, but Cridge ignored all of them.[7]

Belle and her trunk were hustled out into the sunshine, amid a gathering crowd of onlookers. Soldiers who would escort the prisoner to Washington milled around, mingling with Belle's friends and curious townspeople. The crowd's reaction was varied, as evidenced by faces sorrowful, smiling, studied, or triumphant. Lucy Buck observed, "Belle Boyd was taken prisoner and sent off in a carriage with an escort of fifty cavalry men today. I hope she has succeeded in making herself sufficiently notorious now."[8] (Belle claimed the escort consisted of 450 cavalry.[9])

Despite her fear of Cridge and the unknown future, which could hold lengthy imprisonment or even the gallows, the eighteen-year-old betrayed no emotion, even upon leaving the security of Front Royal.

> I knew how closely I was watched by friend and foe, and I resolved neither to make myself an object of derision to the one, nor of pity to the other. Though my heart was throbbing, my eyes were dry; not a muscle of my face quivered; no outward sign betrayed the conflicting emotions that raged within.[10]

Her trunk strapped to the carriage, and Belle installed inside, Cridge mounted the driver's seat and whipped the horses off. In his hand was a tin case containing the papers he had found in Belle's room.

As they departed, the Federal cavalry gathered around the carriage. Some guards went ahead, others followed behind; some fifty scouts marched on either side of the carriage. The heavy escort was occasioned by fear of Turner Ashby's fiercely loyal cavalry. Ashby had been killed in June and his men might take the opportunity to get even by attacking the convoy and rescuing Belle. As Louis Sigaud notes, Belle's uncle, Captain Glenn, and his comrade Harry Gilmor "were quite capable of following her captors well into Federal territory in a mad effort to free her."[11]

Belle seethed with outrage and fright. She resented being imprisoned without accusation, hearing, or trial of any kind! How ironic that she should be treated so harshly, with no concern for her civil rights, by the same tender-hearted emancipators who were so ready to fight for the rights of the Negro! Young, alone, facing captivity and perhaps death, in the custody of the insensitive, villainous Cridge, Belle began to feel sorry for herself.

The travel plan was to proceed through Winchester to Martins-burg and there board a train to Washington. When Belle learned of the stop in Winchester, she asked to spend the night with friends. The request was refused.

On the road to Winchester they halted on a high hill that commanded a view of the countryside for several miles. Her escorts used field glasses to spot any unusual activities in the area, particularly signs of Ashby's cavalry. Still suffering from shock and anxiety, Belle was puzzled by the delay. To her agitated psyche, a nearby large maple tree, with its long and sturdy limbs, loomed as a "hanging tree," perhaps for her. But with nothing untoward on the horizon, the march proceeded.

Upon reaching the outskirts of Winchester they joined the remainder of the regiment that was to escort them through the town. Now some 550 soldiers comprised the caravan. They marched in solemn procession down the main street to the curiosity of Winchester's citizens, and arrived around dinner time at General Julius White's headquarters just beyond the town.[12]

Earlier that day White had wired Assistant Secretary of War Wolcott for instructions: "Mr. Cridge is here with Miss Boyd as prisoner. What shall be done with her?"

Wolcott wired back: "Direct Cridge to come immediately to Washington and bring with him Belle Boyd in close custody, committing her on arrival to the Old Capitol Prison. Furnish him such aid as he may need to get her safely here."[13]

Belle descended from the carriage at White's office and was immediately ushered into the General's presence. White received her with a graceful bow and Belle immediately asked what he intended to do with her.

"Tomorrow I shall send you on to the commanding officer in Martinsburg. He can best inform you what is to be done with you. You will rest here for the night."

"But surely you will at least allow me to remain with my friends in the village until morning?" Belle protested.

"No, no, I cannot consent to that. It would take a whole regiment to guard you; for, though the rebel cavalry should not enter the town to attempt your rescue, I make no doubt that the citizens themselves would try it."

Belle pleaded, "But surely, you do not mean that I should sleep here, defenseless and alone in a tent, at the mercy of your brigade? I never yet slept in a tent when I was present with our army, and how can I endure such a penance in the camp of my enemies?"

White was prepared for that one: "My own tent has been properly prepared for the reception of a lady. Whenever you wish to retire you can follow your inclinations; and you may rest assured you shall sleep in perfect security."[14]

Supper was then served at a fine table and, as Belle looked at the silver and china, she remembered the stories of goods confiscated from Virginia homes. They dined in silence, each lost in thought. As dinner ended White rang for a servant. "Show this lady to the tent which has been prepared for her reception." The servant escorted Belle to the tent and left. She sat on a camp stool, weary and thoughtful, her burdens heavier than she could bear. The sentries paced outside. Soon fatigue overcame her and she slept.

About 3:30 A.M. the camp was abruptly roused by the reports of several muskets fired in quick succession. There followed drum cadences and the piercing staccato of a bugle. Half-dressed officers sprang to arms, rushed to their horses, and rode to their posts. Belle's heart beat rapidly, daring to hope that this was an attempt by the Confederates to rescue her. She hastily lit a candle and sat on her camp stool, anxiously awaiting developments. One officer, as he rushed by, stopped in front of her tent and shouted: "Put out that light; it is a signal to the rebels. Do you hear me?"

Belle obeyed. A few minutes afterwards the drums signaled the end of the disturbance. Belle sought a sentry. What had happened? It seemed that a cow had strayed from a neighboring farm and, not understanding the command of the sentry, had disregarded the order to halt. The soldier, unable to distinguish the figure of the cow in the darkness, fired. Other sentries fired also. When they discovered their foolish mistake they quietly retired to their tents. (The cow was reportedly uninjured.)[15]

At dawn Belle was awakened and ordered to prepare for the trip to Martinsburg. They departed with a reduced escort of about 200 soldiers, stopping for a hearty breakfast at a small farmhouse, a custom of soldiers in enemy territory.

They arrived in Martinsburg shortly after noon. Major Sherman, who had originally accompanied Cridge to arrest Belle, dropped behind the cavalcade and prevailed on his wife to accompany Belle to the camp which lay a short distance north of the town. Upon reaching the camp, Belle was taken immediately to the commanding officer. Could she remain with her family in her own home in Martinsburg while they waited for the train to Washington? It was a reasonable request, and it would have been granted had it not been for Cridge, who replied simply, "Impossible." He insisted that Secretary Stanton would take exception to such an indulgence because it would give Belle an opportunity to communicate with the enemy. Ironically, while she could not visit her home, Cridge could and did, searching for any documents that might give information to the Confederates.

Late that afternoon, as Belle sat at the entrance to her tent, a carriage drove into the encampment. A lady, dressed in mourning with a heavy black veil, stepped out. The mourning costume was but a disguise to afford the wearer access to the camp and Belle recognized her mother at once. With a cry of joy, she ran to her and fell into her arms. Mrs. Boyd renewed the plea that Belle might be allowed to wait in her home, but her elaborate and dramatic effort did not succeed, and again the request was refused. Mrs. Boyd and Major Sherman finally reached a compromise; Belle could go to a hotel and, under guard, stay until time for departure.

Belle was transferred from the camp to Raemer's Hotel next to the railroad station. Upon entering the hotel, accompanied by her mother and Major Sherman's wife, she noticed soldiers stationed everywhere. Sentries were in the lobby, on the stairways, in the halls, in the passage leading to her room, and even just outside her bedroom door. With all these guarantees of her security and good behavior, members of her family (her mother, little sister, and two brothers) were allowed to visit her.

The detective who arrested Belle was to accompany her to Washington, but Belle was so angry with the odious Cridge that she sent for Colonel Holt, Union officer on duty in Martinsburg, imploring him to substitute someone else to guard her on the train. Holt concurred, and Lieutenant Steele of Major Sherman's 12th Illinois Cavalry was detailed for "escort duty."

Belle and her escorts awaited the two A.M. train to Washington. She had maintained her self-control until the time came to leave her family. However, when the Baltimore and Ohio train approached in the distance, she gave way to an outburst of grief, sobbing uncontrollably and partially fainting. She later had no memory of arriving at the station, boarding the train, nor any of the details of her departure. She knew only that she was leaving her loved ones, her home, and all that was dear to her, and that henceforth she would be at the mercy of enemy strangers.

Martinsburg receded into the distance and the darkness outside forced a certain coziness upon her and her captors. She took comfort from the presence of Lieutenant Steele, an officer of apparent decency, to whom she could reasonably look for protection. But her comfort abruptly faded as she looked across the aisle to her left, directly at Detective Cridge. Would she never see the last of this man? Steele did not know that Belle was to be imprisoned and he tried to place her at ease, bringing water to drink and a pillow. He suggested that, on arrival in Washington, she should go to the Willard Hotel for a short rest. He would then call for her and escort her to the office of Secretary Stanton.

In the early morning, about daylight, the train reached the capital. Belle and Lieutenant Steele disembarked and walked toward the station, amazed at the number of people who were waiting at such an early hour to glimpse the "wonderful rebel." Some came in sympathy, some to scoff. As Belle and Steele tried to push through the throng, another officer approached and seized Belle. He was Chief of Detectives LaFayette C. Baker, sent by Stanton to take personal charge of her. "I'm Lafe Baker, Chief of Detectives. Come on, I'll attend to you."[16]

He behaved roughly, shoving her through the crowd. Lieutenant Steele protested vehemently, declaring that Belle was a "lady" and was not to be treated in such a barbarous manner. He begged permission to accompany her to prison. Baker gruffly refused.

Outside the station Baker thrust Belle into a carriage and they began the short ride to the Old Capitol Prison. In the distance she could see the capitol building (still unfinished) which evoked many memories. Soon they saw the vast brick prison, with its thick walls and narrow windows, utterly repulsive. People in the street and inmates of the prison watched as Belle got out of the carriage and entered the prison gates. Some cheered and others jeered. With an air of superiority, Belle held her head high, looking neither to right nor left. Belle reflected,

> Such is the calm retreat provided by a free and enlightened community for those of its citizens who have the audacity to express their disapproval of the policy adopted by the Government of the hour.[17]

However, her proud demeanor masked a frightened creature who sensed she was leaving her childhood outside the gates and entering into a new and fearsome world.

CHAPTER TWELVE

The Old Capitol Prison

31 JULY 1862

Stone walls do not a prison make,
Nor iron bars a cage;
A free and quiet mind can take
These for a hermitage.[1]

THE OLD CAPITOL PRISON was located on Washington's A and 1st streets, near the site of the present Supreme Court building. This long, three-story structure of dingy brick had once been the United States Capitol building, giving the penal institution its name. It had housed the old Congress temporarily after the British had burned the original capitol in 1814. When Congress moved to its permanent headquarters, the old building became a boarding house, patronized by many House and Senate members.

The building then became a makeshift jail, with no effort made toward restoring the structure nor to adapting it to its new function. Decayed walls, creaking doors, broken window panes, rickety stairways, rattling windows, cracked floors, and a dark, gloomy interior indeed made it a domicile for criminals. The bedrooms were notorious for their lice and bedbugs.[2]

Old Capitol cuisine consisted mostly of pork, potatoes, beans, and rice. Some of the prisoners had special privileges and enjoyed choice food and gifts from friends outside. If they had money they could purchase whiskey, tobacco, and other luxuries.[3]

The Old Capitol Prison was intended for political prisoners and prisoners of war, but it soon housed an assortment of inmates including spies, smugglers, and blockade runners. Despite its sorry state, the jail was a sociable place; a rule forbade communication among prisoners but the building was so crowded that separation of inmates was impossible. There was a great deal of card-playing, poker, and other games. Smoking, drinking, and singing enlivened the days and evenings.[4]

When Edwin M. Stanton was made Secretary of War, he was given jurisdiction over the Old Capitol. William P. Wood, the prison superintendent, reported to Stanton and had great influence with the War Department. In fact, it was commonly said in Washington that "Stanton was the head of the war office, and Wood was the head of Stanton."[5]

Superintendent Wood had great physical strength and often used force in disciplining the prisoners. Belle described him as "a man of medium height, powerfully built, with brown hair, fair complexion, and keen bluish-gray eyes."[6] Though rude and uncouth, he could be courteous and obliging when it was to his advantage.

General William E. Doster, who was the Provost Marshal of the District of Columbia at the time, described Wood as "short, ugly, slovenly in dress, in manner affecting stupidity and humility, but at bottom the craftiest of men. He could, and sometimes did, treat his prisoners with respect; he often pretended to be their friend."[7]

Doster also described Belle as he knew her in prison. "Belle Boyd was a lively, spirited young lady, full of caprices, and a genuine rebel. In person she was tall, with light hair and blue eyes. Her features were too irregular to be pretty. It was her dashing manner . . . and air of joyous recklessness which made her interesting. . . . During her whole stay she was never, to my knowledge, found in ill-humor, but bravely endured a tedious and companionless imprisonment."[8]

On entering the prison, Belle was ushered into a small office where a clerk told her to be seated. Soon Superintendent Wood appeared, greeting Belle cordially. "And so this is the celebrated rebel spy! I am very glad to see you, and will endeavor to make you as comfortable as possible; so whatever you wish for, ask for it, and you shall have it. I am glad to have so distinguished a personage for my guest. Come, let me show you to your room."[9]

Wood promised Belle a servant and that she would not be locked in as long as she "behaved herself." He took her across the hall, up the stairs, down a corridor, and left her in room number six. Repeating that she should ask for anything she wished, he withdrew and left her to her thoughts.

Belle closed the door as Wood departed and studied her accommodations: a bed, washstand, table, mirror, and two chairs. Two barred windows highlighted the dingy room, with its cracked plaster walls. Her view included Pennsylvania Avenue which brought memories of happier days. In the distance she could see the former home of General John B. Floyd, Secretary of War in the Buchanan administration.[10] She remembered her many visits in that home as a schoolgirl in Baltimore and when she made her debut into Washington society. That house held many memories of dinners, dances, parties, dates, and congenial friends.

Her reverie was interrupted as a soldier entered and handed her an uninteresting-looking document titled *Rules and Regulations*. She leafed indifferently through the brief treatise, wryly noting one rule in particular: "No communication whatever with fellow prisoners." Not exactly her style![11]

Superintendent Wood had offered her whatever she wanted, so she decided to test his tolerance by calling for a rocking chair and a fire. Despite the rather warm July day, she imagined that the sight of a bright blaze might make her lodgings more cheerful. Wood was true to his word and soon a crackling fire brightened the room.

Belle's trunk was sent up after it had been thoroughly searched; apparently Cridge's earlier examination had not been sufficient. As she leisurely unpacked and arranged her belongings, a sentry was stationed in front of her door.

Soon dinner was served and Belle mentally prepared herself for the bread and water diet that was not uncommon in Civil War prisons. She was startled to discover that her bill of fare was supplemented by goodies from admirers, with fresh fruit and vegetables gracing her tray, as well as the regular meat and potatoes served to other prisoners.

At eight o'clock that evening Superintendent Wood reappeared, accompanied by Chief of Detectives Lafe Baker, who was to interview Belle on behalf of the Secretary of War. Baker expected an easy interview, that Belle would be intimidated and repentant. Baker went straight to the point: "Ain't you pretty tired of your prison a'ready? I've come to get you to make a free confession now of what you've did agin our cause; and, as we've got plenty of proof agin you, you might as well acknowledge at once."

Belle coolly replied, "Sir, I have nothing to say. When you have informed me on what grounds I have been arrested, and given me a copy of the charges preferred against me, I will make my statement; but I shall not now commit myself." Baker scowled and thrust at her a copy of the Oath of Allegiance to the United States of America. He harangued her at some length on the enormity of her crimes and explained that the cause of the South was hopeless. "Say now, won't you take the oath of allegiance? Remember that Mr. Stanton will hear all this. He sent me here."[12]

Eyes aglitter, Belle replied, "Tell Mr. Stanton from me, I hope that when I commence the oath of allegiance to the United States Government, my tongue may cleave to the roof of my mouth; and that if ever I sign one line that will show to the world that I owe the United States Government the slightest allegiance, I hope my arm may fall paralyzed by my side."

Baker stared at her a moment, burning slowly. "Well, if this is your resolution, you'll have to lay here and die; and serve you right."

Belle held her head proudly. "Sir, if it is a crime to love the South, its cause, and its president, then I am a criminal. I am in your power; do with me as you please. But I fear you not. I would rather lie down in this prison and die, than leave it owing allegiance to such a government as yours. Now leave the room; for so thoroughly am I disgusted with your conduct towards me, that I cannot endure your presence longer."

"Bravo! Bravo!" came the cries from every direction. Belle's door had been left open during the exchange, enabling other inmates on the floor to hear. Wood tactfully defused the situation, saying to detective Baker, "Come, we had better go, the lady is tired."[13]

Since it was the detective whom Belle denounced and not Superintendent Wood, the latter was amused. He enjoyed the spectacle and was delighted with Belle's fiery response. In fact, Wood was as captivated by her performance as were the other prisoners. He grew to favor her and the feeling became mutual: "I can safely aver that, beneath his rough exterior, there beats a warm and generous heart," she noted.[14]

A few minutes after Wood and Baker departed, Belle heard a significant cough and a small, white object fell at her feet. Picking it up, she discovered a little nutshell basket upon which small Confederate flags were painted. Wrapped about it was a paper, bearing the words "Courage, You are among friends." It came from an Englishman who had been imprisoned for his Southern sympathies. Belle scribbled a hasty reply and returned it.

Having had quite a day, Belle was exhausted and fell upon her bed. However, the incident with Baker had aroused her too much, and her mind continued to dwell on her dangerous situation. She arose and walked to a window, watching the city in the peaceful moonlight. She yearned for freedom to move and breathe, and the active life she had known. The slumbering city had a restlessness about it, while by contrast, the distant open country, clearly visible in the moonlight, looked the image of peace and repose.

"God made the country, and man made the town," she mused as she contrasted the atmosphere of the prison with the clear air of the fields beyond. She yearned to exchange the sounds of the prison, especially the march of the sentry outside her door, for the shriek of the owl and the rustle of leaves in the wind. But fatigue finally overtook her and again she retired, this time to a tranquil sleep.

> I then lay down on my bed in a tranquil—I had almost said a happy—frame of mind; and I closed my first day in a dungeon by repeating to myself, more than once—
>
> > Stone walls do not a prison make,
> > Nor iron bars a cage;
> > A free and quiet mind can take
> > Those for a hermitage.[15]

✍ CHAPTER THIRTEEN ❧

Prison Snapshots

1-28 AUGUST 1862

I've seen men, when she was singing,
walk off to one side, and pull out their handkerchiefs,
and wipe their eyes,
for fear someone would see them doing the baby act.[1]

ON THE MORNING FOLLOWING her imprisonment, Belle was abruptly awakened by a loud knocking on her door. Alarmed, she cried out, "What is it?"

"The officer calling the roll, to ascertain that no one has escaped."

"You do not expect me to get through these iron bars, do you?" snapped Belle.

"No indeed!"

Belle listened to the officer's retreating footsteps, collected herself, and dressed quickly, relieved that it had been only a false alarm. Soon after, a servant arrived with breakfast and the morning papers. A few minutes later the changing of the guard occurred, with a new sentry installed outside her door. Belle overheard his orders: "You will not allow this lady to come outside her door or talk to any of those fellows in the room opposite; and if she wants anything, call the corporal of the guard. Now don't let these ____ rebels skear yer."[2]

Belle smiled to herself and turned to her breakfast and the day's newspapers. Each paper contained an account of her capture and a summary of her career with diverse assessments of her motives and character. By this time she was learning to tolerate such articles and to accept her circumstances in prison.

Belle's intense patriotism and impertinence had aroused respect and devotion in her fellow prisoners. They slipped her candy, fruit, flowers, and small Confederate flags, feeding well this eighteen-year-old's hunger for reassurance. And yet, deep down, she was frightened, a young fawn in a strange zoo. She paced the floor at night, dwelling on her predicament.

Belle's cell had been a committee room of the old congress, used by Clay, Webster, Calhoun, and other statesmen of their generation. "The list of prominent names on the walls of Belle's room could compete in length and respectability with the registers of the best and largest hotels," observes Louis Sigaud.[3]

The history of the past rose before her. "I fancied I could hear the voices of departed orators as they declaimed against the abuses and errors of their day."[4] She imagined the Hayne-Webster debates as the nature of the Union was argued and Calhoun as he presented his views on states' rights and nullification. She could hear the endless debates over secession, expansion of slavery to the territories, abolition, and the status of fugitive slaves. Her imagination envisioned Daniel Webster giving his famous 7th of March speech supporting the Compromise of 1850. He was willing to make a compromise with slavery in order to preserve the Union: "Theirs was the bright day— ours is the dark morrow, of which the evil is more than sufficient."[5]

Aside from want of exercise, she suffered no physical privations, and read, wrote, and sewed. She enjoyed her meals, served by the sentry who guarded her door. In time, even the sentry succumbed to Belle's magnetism and passionate personality, and passed messages in and out of the prison for her. One visitor remarked that, when he called on her, she was reading *Harpers* and eating peaches, and told him that she could afford to remain in the Old Capitol as long as Stanton could afford to keep her.[6]

The Old Capitol ban on communications among prisoners somehow did not apply very well to Belle. She soon learned to use the knife on her food tray to dig finger-sized holes in the plaster walls, holes large enough for the transmission of notes. Such clandestine correspondence was a source of pleasure and "served to beguile many a tedious hour."[7]

When sitting in her doorway, as she was sometimes permitted, prisoners crowded the doors and stairsteps for a glimpse of her face and an opportunity to hear her voice as she treated them to a concert of patriotic songs. She sometimes led them in singing "Dixie" and other folk songs of the South.

Her favorite song, and certainly that of the prisoners, was "Maryland, My Maryland," widely considered to be one of the greatest American Civil War lyrics. James Ryder Randall wrote it, inspired by the first bloodletting of the war, which occurred in Baltimore on 19 April 1861 as volunteers of the 6th Massachusetts Regiment provoked a riot by passing through the city. The verses were published on 31 May and the song became immediately popular as the "Marseillaise" of the South.[7]

One of the prisoners who heard Belle sing was Gus Williams from Vienna, Virginia.[8] One day after Belle was released, he heard some of the boys singing "Maryland, My Maryland" and strolled over to express his opinion:

> I've heard "Maryland, My Maryland" sung here in the old building in a way that would make you feel like jumping out of the window and swimming across the Potomac. . . . Belle Boyd . . . would sing that song as if her very soul was in every word she uttered. It used to bring a lump up in my throat every time I heard it. It seemed like my heart was ready to jump out—as if I could put my fingers down and touch it. I've seen men, when she was singing, walk off to one side, and pull out their handkerchiefs, and wipe their eyes, for fear someone would see them doing the baby act.[9]

When Belle attended Sunday morning worship services at the prison, her companions noted that "she walked with a grace and dignity which might be envied by a queen." She shook hands with her fellow prisoners and they tipped their hats to her. The Northern prisoners stared enviously. A fellow-prisoner noted,

> . . . on Sundays, when there was preaching down in the yard, she would be allowed to come down and sit near the preacher. If you could only have seen how the fellows would try to get near her as she passed. And if she gave them a look or a smile, it did them more good than the preaching. You wouldn't hear a cuss word from any of them for a week, even if one of the guards would swear at them or threaten them.[10]

Most of the prisoners passed Belle's door on their way to their half-hour of recreation outdoors. Among them were old friends and acquaintances, most of whom had served in the Confederate army in Virginia. Belle soon learned to be very discreet in communicating with anyone she knew. One day she had encountered her cousin, John Stephenson, a young officer in John S. Mosby's cavalry. She was so glad to see him that she rushed up and excitedly exchanged a few words with him. But a sentry stopped her with his bayonet and sent her to her room. The unfortunate cousin was removed to the guard room and she did not see him again.[11]

As the only woman in the prison, and a young and famous one at that, she was the hub of attention and thoroughly enjoyed it. But prison was prison and she grew bored with the lack of activity. Outdoor life and horseback riding were her constitutional necessities and she begged permission to walk outdoors, accompanied by an officer. The otherwise cooperative Wood refused, by orders from Stanton.[12]

On the fourth morning of her imprisonment, she watched from her door as other prisoners passed by on their way to breakfast. One of them slipped to her a half-length portrait of Jefferson Davis, evidently smuggled into the prison. Belle defiantly hung the picture in her room above the mantelpiece, with this inscription below it:

Three cheers for Jeff Davis and the Southern Confederacy!

Upon seeing the picture a prison official rushed into the room, confiscated the portrait, and locked the door.[13]

Belle's offense was severely punished by several weeks of confinement to her locked room. It was a very hot August, and little air stirred, so that she became weak and dizzy. Superintendent Wood noted her paleness and relented, ordering that her door be left open. Soon afterward he granted her a daily half-hour's walk in the prison yard, accompanied by a guard.[14]

Belle became very friendly with fellow-prisoner Dennis A. Mahony, a newspaper editor from Dubuque, Iowa. She learned that his only offense against the Union was, ironically, in upholding the Constitution. A fierce believer in freedom of speech and opinion, he expressed his beliefs in his newspaper, fearlessly denouncing certain Federal policies. As a result, all of his property, including his newspaper, was seized without due process of law and he was sent to the Old Capitol.[15]

Belle felt pity as she watched Mr. Mahony, "almost bent double with age, his long white hair hung down to his shoulders, while his beard (gray with the touch of Old Father Time's fingers) reached nearly to his waist." Mahony wrote *The Prisoner of State* to protest his treatment, and devoted many pages to the young rebel woman who gave him sympathy:

> Among the prisoners in the Old Capitol when I reached there was the somewhat famous Belle Boyd, to whom has been attributed the defeat of General Banks, in the Shenandoah Valley, by Stonewall Jackson. Belle, as she is familiarly called by all the prisoners, and affectionately so by the Confederates, was arrested and imprisoned as a spy. . . .
>
> The first intimation some of us newcomers in the Old Capitol had of the fact of there being a lady in that place was the hearing of "Maryland, My Maryland", sung the first night of our incarceration, in what we could not be mistaken was a woman's voice. On inquiry, we were informed that it was Belle Boyd. Some of us had never heard of the lady before; and we were all inquiring about her. Who was she? Where was she from? And what did she do? . . .
>
> Belle was in solitary confinement, but allowed to have her room door open, and to sit outside of it in a hall or stair-landing in the evening. Whenever she availed herself of this privilege, as she frequently did, the greatest curiosity was manifested by the victims of despotism to see her. Her room being on the second story; those who occupied the third story were civilians from Fredericksburg. . . .
>
> But we must not lose sight of Belle Boyd. I heard her voice, my first night in prison, singing "Maryland, My Maryland", the first time I had ever heard the Southern song. The words, stirring enough to Southern hearts, were enunciated by her with such peculiar expression as to touch even the sensibilities which did not sympathize with the cause which inspired the song. It was difficult to listen unmoved to this lady, throwing her whole soul, as it were, into the expression of the sentiments of devotion to the South, defiance to the

North, and affectionately confident appeals to Maryland, which form the burden of that celebrated song. The pathos of her voice, her apparently forlorn condition, and, at those times when her soul seemed absorbed in the thoughts she was uttering in song, her melancholy manner, affected all who heard her, not only with compassion for her, but with an interest in her which came near, on several occasions, bringing about a conflict between the prisoners and the guards.

Fronting on the same hall or stair-landing on which Belle Boyd's room-door opened, were three other rooms, all filled to their capacity with prisoners, mostly Confederate officers. Several of those were personally acquainted with Belle, as she was most of the time, and by nearly every one, called. In the evenings these prisoners were permitted to crowd inside of their room-doors, whence they could see and sometimes exchange a word with Belle. When this liberty was not allowed, she contrived to procure a large marble, around which she would tie a note written on tissue-paper, and, when the guard turned his back to patrol his beat in the hall, she would roll the marble into one of the open doors of the Confederate prisoners' rooms. When the contents were read and noted a missive would be written in reply, and the marble . . . would be rolled back to Belle.[16]

It would be very misleading to leave the impression that Belle's stint in the Old Capitol was all sweetness and light. On one occasion a servant brought her a loaf of sugar and it occurred to her to share it with the officers in the room across the hall. She asked a sentry's permission to pass it over to them, and the sentry said, "I have no objection."

But then, inexplicably, as Belle was placing the sugar in the hands of the officers, the sentry struck her left hand with the end of his musket. The violent blow broke her thumb and the pain was so great and sudden that she burst into tears. Again, inexplicably, the sentry pinned her to the wall by her dress, his musket inflicting a flesh wound on her arm. A guard rushed up the stairs and saw her predicament; the sentry was removed from his post and sent to the guard room. Her fellow inmates were so enraged by the incident that, had Belle been seriously hurt, the sentry probably would have been torn to pieces.[17]

Even in prison, Belle was causing grief for the Union. On 6 August 1862, President Lincoln and other high officials addressed a large crowd in front of the Capitol. A woman in the audience disrupted the event and was arrested for making a pro-Southern outburst. Held for questioning, she said that she wanted to meet with Belle Boyd and admitted frequently passing the prison, hoping for a glimpse of the Rebel Spy. Although she denied actually communicating with Belle, she admitted that her husband had visited the prisoner.[18]

On the day that the *Washington Star* reported this incident, the War Department began an investigation. In a letter authorized by Secretary Stanton, Assistant Secretary of War Watson wrote to the District Military Commandant, General Wadsworth, complaining that his order to keep the Rebel Spy in close custody had been violated.[19]

Wadsworth replied on the same day with a detailed report. He denied receiving the "close-custody" order, but noted that Superintendent Wood was aware of it and had let people in to see Belle anyway.[20] This demonstrated not only the communication problems in the War Department, but Wood's disregard for Stanton as well.

An interesting fellow-prisoner of Belle's was the "Boy Spy," Joseph O. Kerbey. He had landed in prison because, even though he was a Union spy, he had refused to take an oath of allegiance to the United States government. The Boy Spy had been a student of telegraphy and as such had been called into the service of the Union to intercept telegraphed Confederate communiques. As an employee of the Secret Service he was obliged to take the oath of allegiance but his conscience would not allow him to do so. Consequently, Stanton ordered him sent to the Old Capitol Prison, where he spent three weeks in the late summer of 1862.

Belle met Kerbey on the first morning of his imprisonment. "I was anxious to see who it was that was here by Stanton's express orders," she told him. "I was in Wood's office last evening, and heard him tell the officer on duty that 'the new prisoner is here, under Mr. Stanton's orders.' I'm glad to know that you are among friends now!"

The Boy Spy was surprised to learn that the young woman was "Belle Boyd, the celebrated female spy." He knew of her daring exploits in the Shenandoah Valley with Stonewall Jackson and Jeb Stuart. Belle was slightly his senior and to him she suggested "a spirit from another world." He described her as " . . . a neatly dressed young lady, with a lithe and graceful figure. . . . She was of a light, rather fair complexion; her hair was a strawberry blonde; while she was not strictly a handsome woman, there was something in her manner that was very attractive."[21]

Even though Kerbey was a Union spy, Belle befriended him and they even collaborated on a plan for his escape. As it happened, he was released from the Old Capitol before they made the attempt, and went on to distinguish himself with the rank of Major in the Federal Army.[22]

One very romantic story, oddly omitted by Belle from her diary, was her courtship and engagement to a Confederate officer, Lieutenant Clifford McVay of Virginia. Badly injured when he came to the prison, he was placed in the cell diagonally across the hall from Belle. She had likely met him previously, during her "coming out" parties in Washington.

The two now found themselves together in prison. Their past experiences and present plight drew them together. She does not reveal the circumstances of their meeting in prison, nor her true feelings toward him. We only know that whenever they were allowed, they sat together in the prison yard or talked across the hallway. The otherwise romantic Belle is silent about the event, except for mentioning a possible wedding outfit![23]

William E. Doster, Provost Marshal and friend of Lincoln, gives an interesting account about the wedding outfit. Once, when he called on Belle, she said that there was so little do do in prison that she found it was an excellent chance to brush up on her literature and to get her wedding outfit ready. . . . She said that she was engaged to marry an officer of the Rebel army and wanted to buy her trousseau in Washington before leaving, but Stanton would not listen to the suggestion. However— "after she arrived in Richmond she sent a schedule of the articles she wanted to Mr. Wood, the superintendent, who, I understood, forwarded them to her under a flag of truce."[24]

While Belle actually got her trousseau, she did not marry Lieutenant McVay, and there is nothing to indicate what happened to him.[25]

Mahony wrote that McVay was "a handsome and dashing gentleman." Many of the prisoners envied McVay his good fortune, although, as far as is known, their romance was restricted to rolling marbles back and forth with notes wrapped around them. It was a game they played across the corridor in view of all, behind the backs of the guards. In this they had plenty of help in signals given by the other prisoners.[26]

Belle's final anecdote on the Old Capitol is about Superintendent Wood. One Sunday morning he came stalking down the hall, proclaiming in the tones of a medieval town crier: "All you who want to hear the word of God preached according to Jeff Davis go down into the yard; and all you who want to hear it preached according to Abe Lincoln go into No. 16 [where some Union prisoners were held].[27]

CHAPTER FOURTEEN

You Are Going to Dixie Tomorrow!

28 AUGUST—1 SEPTEMBER 1862

She left soon after I came in.
I was glad to know that she was released,
but we all missed her. Even some of the Yankees,
although they would not show it while she was here;
but when she was sent away they missed her
sweet singing—Rebel songs though they were.
One of them told me it made him feel
sad to hear her sing.
—Prison Life in the Old Capitol[1]

"**A**LL YOU REBELS get ready! You are going to Dixie tomorrow and Miss Belle is going with you!" yelled Superintendent Wood.[2]

Belle, reading by her open door on that sultry evening of 28 August, could scarcely believe her ears and screamed with joy at the news. The prisoners cheered and the remainder of the evening was spent in rejoicing and celebration, hurried farewells, and general bedlam.

It was not until early the following morning that the noise and excitement subsided. During the joyful night Belle's fellow-prisoners passed the hat to buy a gift for their favorite rebel, a gift that would be delivered after her arrival in Richmond.

What had happened? Why, so suddenly, were the rebel prisoners, and particularly an espionage agent like Belle, being set free? The reason was simple: The Federal and Confederate Governments had arranged for a formal exchange of prisoners and this event at the Old Capitol was the first result.

HEADQUARTERS MILITARY DISTRICT
OF WASHINGTON,
Washington, D.C.,
August 29, 1862.

Major General Dix, Fort Monroe.

GENERAL: I am directed by General Thomas to forward to you all of the prisoners of war now confined in the
Old Capitol Prison. Inclosed herewith are lists of the prisoners forwarded. I forward likewise *Miss Belle Boyd,* a young
lady arrested on suspicion of having communicated with the
enemy. I have agreed that she shall be placed over the lines
by the first flag of truce, which is in accordance with her
wishes. No specific charge or information have been lodged
against her.

I have the honor to be, very respectfully, your obedient
servant,

JAMES S. WADSWORTH,
Brigadier-General, etc.[3]

The happy tumult in the Old Capitol that night was probably
matched in some Southern prison where Union inmates joyously
prepared for their release the next morning. In all likelihood, the
Federals were glad to be rid of Belle, whose presence boosted prisoner
morale in the Old Capitol, for her situation was daily discussed in the
press, and her spunky partisan pride in the South was widely admired.

SPECIAL ORDERS, HDQRS. MILITARY
DIST. OF WASHINGTON
No. 175. Washington, D.C.,
August 29, 1862.

V. All prisoners of war now in confinement in Old
Capitol Prison desirous of being exchanged will be forthwith
sent to the transport Juniata, foot of Sixth street, to be taken
to Fortress Monroe [near Norfolk]. The provost-marshal will
immediately detail one competent commissioned officer and
twenty men to take charge of these prisoners. The officer so
detailed will on his arrival at Fortress Monroe report to
Major-General Dix, commanding. He will also take charge of

Miss Belle Boyd, now confined in Old Capitol Prison, and turn her over to Major-General Dix to be sent through the lines to the south.

By command of Brigadier-General Wadsworth:
JOHN P. SHERBURNE,
Assistant Adjutant-General.[4]

The next morning the 200 rebel exchangees lined up in the courtyard, marched through the prison gates, across the street, and queued up for departure. Belle walked to an open carriage, accompanied by Major Norman Fitzhugh, who had instructions to take her to Richmond.[5]

Belle bade a tender farewell to her fellow prisoners and newspaperman Mahony wrote that there was not a man from the prison who failed to be overcome by his emotions.[6] As Belle's carriage pulled away, her fellow-prisoners cheered loudly. Some Washingtonians, who had gathered to view the departure, applauded so vehemently that the whole street and square resounded. Belle's mood was a mixture of pleasure and sadness: pleasure at the prospect of freedom, and sadness at the thought of leaving Clifford McVay behind.[7]

Carl Sandburg noted,

On the evidence she could have been legally convicted as a spy, shot at sunrise and heard of no more, but she became one of two hundred prisoners who were exchanged and sent to Richmond.[8]

The journey by water from Washington to Richmond was a long and tedious one. The *Juniata* sailed at dawn on 30 August, proceeding down the Potomac to the mouth of the river where they passed the night. At dawn on the 31st they sailed down Chesapeake Bay, arriving at Fortress Monroe late in the evening. On each side of the *Juniata* lay General McClellan's transports, filled with soldiers, preparing for the attack on Richmond. Despite the danger, the ex-prisoners on the *Juniata* cut loose with rebel songs, interspersed with loud cheers for Jefferson Davis. Belle's voice rose clearly among those of the soldiers.[9]

The ship resumed the last portion of the journey, up the muddy waters of the James River toward Richmond. As they rounded a bend, a Confederate flag became visible, waving from a window in the home of a Mr. Aikens, a friend of the Boyd family. The impact upon Belle and her companions was electric. Only then did they fully feel that they were really free and going home! Their earlier cheers were nothing as compared to their shouts upon seeing the Stars and Bars. Again they burst into song, finishing with "Dixie". Belle was proud that she had not been cowed by the Union and that she had not given in to Stanton. Prison life had not crushed her spirit—it had only strengthened it![10]

At a wharf near Richmond the *Juniata* was met by Colonel Robert Ould, the Confederate Commissioner for Exchange of Prisoners, and his assistant, a Mr. Watson. Under their supervision the exchanged prisoners were marched ashore. Belle was allowed to spend the evening and night at the Aikens home and once again she enjoyed the hospitality for which the South was famous.[11]

But what of Belle's fiancé, Lieutenant McVay, who remained in prison? He was scheduled to be sent south at some indefinite time and they had hoped to be married after their release. But she never saw him again as he disappeared completely from her life. Belle is strangely silent concerning his destiny (legend has it that he died during the war). Belle's reticence to write about her Secret Service work may have extended to her private affairs as she wrote nothing of her prison romance.[12]

PART FIVE

Riding High

(1862-1864)

Belle Boyd cottage in Front Royal. (Photo by A. W. Carroll, photographer, and print courtesy of Laura Virginia Hale and the Warren Rifles Confederate Museum, all Front Royal VA.)

Capital of
the Confederacy

2 SEPTEMBER 1862

God bless you, my child!
—General Jackson's farewell to Belle Boyd.[1]

THE NEXT MORNING, a Colonel Allen sent his carriage to take Belle to Richmond. Her journey was a virtual march of triumph. As she passed by the encampment of the Richmond Blues, the august company was drawn up in review and presented arms, swelling her heart with pride and pleasure from the high compliment.[2]

On arrival in Richmond, Belle went to the Ballard House, one of the finest hotels in the city, where rooms had been reserved for her. That evening she was serenaded by the city band, part of her treatment as a distinguished guest.

From the windows of her hotel room she could see the city below, the capitol building where the Confederate Congress met, and the boats on the James as they passed beneath the bridge. In the distance stood the White House of the Confederacy, its tall columns and Grecian lines perhaps reassuring her of the permanence of the Confederate States of America.[3]

After nearly two weeks at the Ballard House, Belle moved to a boarding house on Grace Street. There she enjoyed the companionship of old friends and met General Joseph E. Johnston, who was recuperating from a wound received at the Battle of Seven Pines. She also met General Louis T. Wigfall of Texas (a Fort Sumter hero and now a Confederate Congressman), and Mrs. John C. Calhoun, widow of the famous senator from South Carolina, "who was equally and justly renowned for her wit and charms."[4]

One evening, an officer who had been a fellow inmate at the Old Capitol Prison visited Belle and presented her with a note and a small box. It was the gift purchased with funds collected at the prison just before her release. The box contained a gold and enamel watch, richly set with diamonds. It was, said the note, a token of their love and esteem.

> For a few moments I could not find words to thank their delegate, so overpowered was I by this striking and unexpected mark of the feelings entertained for me by my countrymen.[5]

While in Richmond Belle bloomed socially and fashionably once again, sporting a new riding costume in which she happily sat on horseback at troop reviews. Her trousseau arrived, purchased by the Old Capitol Prison's Superintendent Wood, and she excited the ladies at the boarding house with her finery. She dressed in fashionable clothes for the benefit of fellow boarders and visitors. Witty and charming, Belle enjoyed the expensive luster of the debutante again, but her eighteen-year-old heart had been away from home a very long time and she suffered pangs of homesickness, longing to be with her family again.[6]

Martinsburg was again in the hands of the Confederates, making her return a fairly safe prospect, so she contacted her parents and her father soon arrived to take her home. Belle was overcome with emotion upon seeing him—he looked much older and thinner, and walked with a cane. His clothes hung loosely and the small flight of stairs caused him shortness of breath. He was on sick leave, expecting to return to action when he regained his strength.[7]

Upon arrival in Martinsburg they heard the news of the Emancipation Proclamation. President Lincoln had announced that, on 1 January 1863, all slaves in the states of the Confederacy would be set free. The war would now take on a new flavor and fervor—that of a crusade—the "right" of the Southerners to hold slaves, against the "right" of the slaves to be free. Belle, like most Southerners, looked upon this as a war measure, since it applied only to the slaves in the states that had seceded. It did not affect the border states (including the western part of Virginia) where slavery was still allowed![8]

Belle rode to the Confederate encampment outside Martinsburg, escorted by a friend, to pay a call on General Jackson. As she dismounted, Stonewall stepped from his tent and placed his hands on her head. "God bless you, my child!" he exclaimed, praising her achievements and sharing her anger over her imprisonment. He then warned her that, if his army had to leave Martinsburg, she once again would be in great jeopardy. "It will be much worse next time if you are captured," he counselled. "You should leave now, or at least be prepared to flee upon a moment's notice. I will warn you if I must leave." He placed his hands on her head once again and repeated, "God bless you, my child!" This farewell, the last words she would hear from the General's lips, she would treasure always.[9]

Jackson kept his promise. In a few days he sent word to Belle that his troops were preparing for a retreat to Winchester and that she should precede his army, thus keeping friendly forces between herself and the enemy. Since horses of civilians had been confiscated by the enemy, he provided her with transportation and an escort as far as Winchester.

Upon arrival in Winchester she was commissioned a Captain and made an honorary aide-de-camp to Stonewall, a most unusual honor for a woman. On this occasion she was presented with a handsome new riding habit, made of Confederate gray cloth, trimmed in black braid, with the insignia of Captain on the collar. It had a neat, well-fitting jacket, a long riding skirt, and a soft felt hat with a plume. The uniform was a gift of the Confederate Army in appreciation of her heroism and loyalty.[10]

The rank of Captain brought some exciting privileges, one of which was that she be accorded the respect and courtesies enjoyed by officers; another was that she might assist at reviews of troops. She was present when the Southern troops were reviewed by Lord Hartingdon and Colonel Leslie and when General Cadmus Wilcox's division was inspected by Generals Lee and Longstreet, attending on horseback and freely mixing with the staff officers of the several commanders.

For the next few months Belle rode with the dignity and pride of a queen. Although these courtesies were symbols of her new status, they did not change her attitude, kindness of heart, or devotion to duty. She was the Southern Joan of Arc, inspiring the troops.[11]

One incident, related by Myrta Lockett Avary in her diary of the war years, shows Belle's compassion for others. While reviewing troops near Winchester, Belle met a young soldier boy, painfully trudging along on his bare feet. She removed her fine cloth gaiters (ankle-high shoes), which were laced on the side and trimmed with patent leather, and gave them to him. A friend protested, saying that such shoes would not last the boy long enough to justify the sacrifice. But Belle retorted, "Oh, if it rests his poor young feet only a little while, I am repaid. He is not old enough to be away from his mother." Belle then proceeded to the review, unconcerned that her lack of shoes might attract attention and cause comment.[12]

About this time (17 September 1862), the battle of Antietam was fought, General Lee's first incursion into Northern territory and the bloodiest battle of the war. After Antietam the South Carolina brigade, under cavalryman Wade Hampton, joined the Confederate forces in camp at Opequon Creek near Martinsburg. While Hampton was thus stationed, Belle took the opportunity to return home often. On one such occasion she was accompanied by a large party and they quickly improvised a dance. During the evening came the word that the Yankees were coming, but thinking it was a joke—they had heard similar warnings before—they paid no attention. However, this time it was true, and not a cry of "wolf!" When they finally realized the danger, they barely had time to escape before the enemy was upon them.[13]

Belle began to weary of the constant troop reviews, marches, reversals of occupation, and threat of capture. Despite her romantic, frenetic life, she wished to return to Martinsburg and her mother. Remembering Stonewall's warning, she wrote him for advice.

> Headquarters, Army of Virginia,
> Near Culpepper Court-House.

My dear Child,

I received your letter asking my advice regarding your returning to your home, which is now in the Federal lines. As you have asked my advice, I can but candidly give it. I think that it is not safe; and therefore do not attempt it until it is, for you know the consequences. You would doubtless be imprisoned, and possibly not released so soon again. You had better go to your relatives in Tennessee, and there remain until you can go with safety. God bless you!

Truly your friend,
T. J. Jackson[14]

Belle lost no time in following Jackson's advice and promptly departed for Knoxville.

CHAPTER SIXTEEN

Winter in Knoxville

AUTUMN 1862—SPRING 1863

*She seemed to feel the weight
of the Confederacy on her shoulders. . . .*[1]

THUS FAR THE SOUTH was winning the battles in the east. The Union campaign against Richmond had failed and the struggle for the Shenandoah Valley had been checked by Jackson. There were minor Union victories in Tennessee, at Forts Henry and Donaldson, under the leadership of U. S. Grant, whose name would soon become a household word. One major Federal victory was the capture of New Orleans which gave the Union control of the lower Mississippi River as far as Vicksburg.[2] It was during this lull in the war in the east that Belle left for Knoxville.

Up to this point, most descriptions of Belle Boyd had been penned by men, but from the autumn of 1862 we have impressions of her in the diary of a young woman Belle's own age, "Nellie Grey." This was a pseudonym; she was the wife of Confederate Major Joseph H. Nash. Nellie Grey was temporarily residing at a boarding house owned by a Mrs. Rixey in Culpepper, Virginia.[3]

Belle, on her way to Tennessee, stopped at Culpepper where General Lee was assembling his forces. She spent the night at Mrs. Rixey's and it was here that the two young women met. Nellie Grey vividly describes Belle's brief visit in her diary, paraphrased below . . .

It was late October or early November and snow had begun to fall. The Confederates were suffering keenly from the early winter weather, lacking heavy clothing, winter underwear, shoes, and over-coats. Many wrapped blankets around themselves to ward off the cold.

Snow fell heavily as a chilled, tired Belle reached Mrs. Rixey's, in search of food and shelter. She asked for accommodations, but every room was taken. Belle pleaded that she would take anything—even a spare cot in another woman's room. Mrs. Rixey asked Nellie if she would share her room with a lady who had just arrived and she consented.

Nellie then descended to the parlor and was puzzled to find it crowded with soldiers. Mrs. Rixey introduced the new arrival, but Nellie did not catch the name. Nellie described Belle as a girl of about eighteen or twenty, exceedingly well-dressed and rather young to be traveling alone "unless one were married." A "brilliant talker," she had much to tell, and seemed to prefer conversing with men, who clustered about her. She told her listeners that she had recently been released from the Old Capitol Prison and showed them the watch that was her farewell gift from the inmates.

Nellie Grey retired and was asleep when her roommate came upstairs. The following morning they awoke face to face in the same bed. In this bizarre circumstance, Belle introduced herself and, noted Nellie, "I knew for the first time that my bedfellow was the South's most famous spy." If Nellie had any doubt that her companion was a Confederate agent, such doubt was soon dispelled, as Belle proceeded to take her morning bath, producing a large bottle of cologne and emptying the contents into a basin. Such luxuries were available only to a favored few, and foremost among them the daring ones such as blockade runners. "It was the first cologne I had seen for more than a year, and it was the last I saw until I ran the blockade," wrote Nellie.

Nellie Grey's brother-in-law, Richard, came to visit her at Mrs. Rixey's. Although once a "noted dandy," he was now dressed in "miserable and filthy rags and tatters, a most abject and pitiable-looking creature." He was embarrassed to be seen by the ladies and refused to enter the guest-filled dining room.

Belle ignored his shyness and led him in. Nellie confided, "While we held council he had been in Mrs. Rixey's and Miss Boyd's hands, and had had a good dinner." Belle collected clothing for him; one person gave a shirt, another a pair of socks, and another some underwear. As Richard left, Belle came running down the stairs with a large, new blanket shawl and pinned it snugly around his shoulders. He protested that the shawl was too fine and expensive, but Belle replied: "I can't let you go back to camp in this thin jacket while I have this shawl. It is serving our country, Lieutenant, while it protects her soldier from the cold."

But, Richard protested again, Belle might need the shawl.

"I may need it? No, no, I can get others where this came from."

As the ladies watched him go, they saw him remove his shoes, which the army had given him that very morning. They did not fit and his bruised feet could no longer endure them. Nellie commented that, as he left, those who watched were grieved to see that his blood "etched his footprints on the snow."

"She did not spend another night with us. She seemed to feel the weight of the Confederacy on her shoulders, and took the afternoon train to Richmond."[4]

Arriving in Knoxville in late 1862, Belle was warmly welcomed by John and Isabella Boyd, her great uncle and aunt who had moved to Tennessee after their marriage in 1803. Also greeting her was Samuel Boyd, who had left Martinsburg when Belle was a child, and married one of the Tennessee cousins, Isabella Reed Boyd. He had studied law at Blount College (now the University of Tennessee), and returned to Knoxville to pursue his legal career.[5]

For about six months Belle visited numerous kinfolk who welcomed her for long stays. Southern families had a reputation for their gracious hospitality, loving to entertain and be entertained. Landed proprietors had big estates and numerous slaves. The owner lived in a mansion, beautifully furnished, usually in the country, and approached through an avenue of trees. Sometimes the mansion house was located in a nearby town.

The country mansion was typically surrounded by an outdoor kitchen, smokehouse, wash house, barns, chicken houses, a schoolroom, and (a short distance from the house) Negro cabins and a vegetable garden.

These homes were the scene of a delightful social life. Long visits were exchanged between families and friends. Distances were so great and travel so slow that when guests arrived they usually remained for a prolonged visit. Visitors presented no problem as houses were large, servants were many and food was plentiful.[6]

In February 1863, Belle settled in for a lengthy stay with her aunt, Susan Boyd, widow of Judge Samuel Boyd, a former mayor of Knoxville. They lived in the old Blount Mansion, a Knoxville showplace, and the former home of Governor William Blount. News of the Rebel Spy's presence soon spread through the city.[7]

On the second night after her arrival, a huge crowd gathered outside the mansion. After several songs there was a clamor for her to appear on the balcony. Overcome emotionally and oddly shy about making a speech, she was reluctant to appear. General Joseph E. Johnston was also visiting the mansion and Belle appealed to him to substitute for her. He spoke briefly but the crowd below would not be satisfied without a glimpse of Belle. Finally, she steadied her nerves, stepped forth on the balcony, and the shouts nearly doubled.

When silence was restored she addressed the audience with something less than her usual glib loquacity: "Like General Joe Johnston, I can fight, but I cannot make speeches. But, my good friends, I no less feel and appreciate the compliment you have paid me this night."[8]

Brief and plain as the speech was, Belle expressed relief when it was over. The crowd then sang "Dixie" and "Good Night" and faded into the night with the band still playing. Next morning the newspapers gave glowing accounts of the whole affair, no longer calling Belle "the Rebel Spy" but rather the "Virginia heroine."[9]

One of Aunt Susan Boyd's daughters (whose name was also Sue) was the same age as Belle. They grew very close, attending the same parties, riding horseback, and entertaining beaux in the same parlor. In 1932, Sue Boyd (Barton) remembered Belle's visit in a letter.

> . . . Belle Boyd came to Knoxville in the late summer of 1862. After about a six weeks visit with other kinspeople in Knoxville (in the country & in Town) where there were no young people, she grew restless & discontent & threatened to be "on the go" (as she called it). My Mother, who had a large family—both girls & boys—finally prevailed on Belle to spend the Winter & Spring with us in our Home—now the Old "Blount Mansion."
>
> Belle came to us at once & seemed very happy. We knew & loved her Father and Mother—Cousin Ben & Mary Boyd & my Mother realized how anxious & uneasy her

Mother (Cousin Mary Boyd) must be—with a young Daughter out in the World, at such a time, without protection. Our family rules seemed a bit of restraint to her at first. But she soon conformed acceptably to them & was thereby happier.

Belle was homely in face & feature but was very attractive otherwise. She was a witty & brilliant talker; was gracious—graceful & had the most perfect form or figure I ever beheld. She was a fearless & magnificent *Horse Back Rider*; a wonderful dancer; merry & lighthearted seemingly without a care, or responsibility in the world. When she came to us she showed us a handsome "Riding-Habit"—new; made of the grey Confederate cloth & trimmed in black braid, with the rank of "Capt." on the collar. She said it was presented to her by the Confederate Army for her Heroism & Loyalty to the Cause. She was popular with all & especially with the officers & soldier boys who came to our Home. She often told my Mother she was never happier although it was the first time in her life she ever had to conform to Family Rules.

After the Winter & Spring passed, she again grew restless & said she was tired of home-life & wanted something more ex-ci-ting & "new fields to conquer" & left our Home for friends in Ala. & Geo. . . .[10]

A Tour
A Death, and
A Homecoming

SPRING 1863

*These few words were the funeral oration
of a man who, for a rare combination of best
and the greatest qualities,has seldom or never
been surpassed.*[1]

BELLE LEFT TENNESSEE with many happy memories and headed for the deep South. She planned short stops in Alabama, Georgia, and South Carolina, and then a return to Martinsburg if it was safe. Belle does not detail her trip; she does not describe the receptions, nor the cities, plantations, or countryside. Her writing at this point, like her whirl-wind tour, is sketchy and hurried. She says only that:

Invitations of the most hospitable and delicate nature poured in upon me. Offers of assistance and assurances of regard and affection were innumerable. I accepted as many invita-tions as my time would permit, and was rejoiced at the opportunities I enjoyed of going over the famous and produc-tive cotton plantations of Alabama.[2]

Belle visited in Montgomery, capital of Alabama and the original capital of the Confederacy. She then moved on to Mobile and it was here that she received a dreadful telegram:

Battle House, Mobile, Alabama.

Miss Belle Boyd,
General Jackson now lies in state at the Governor's mansion.
T. Bassett French,
Aide-de-camp to the Governor[3]

She was stunned. Before reaching Mobile, she heard a report that he had been wounded in early May, shot by his own men in the confusion and darkness at the battle of Chancellorsville, Virginia. His condition was supposedly not dangerous and it was thought that he would soon be in the saddle again. Belle, like many others, probably felt that nothing could happen to the invincible Jackson—that he would always be there, like a stone wall. In her diary she sadly observed: "These few words [of the telegram] were the funeral oration of a man who, for a rare combination of best and the greatest qualities, has seldom or never been surpassed."[4]

Belle's only outward expression of grief was a band of black crepe that she wore on her left arm for the next thirty days in conformity with military mourning. She was too hurt to even talk about his death and states that she would "leave it to more capable writers to describe the career and virtues of General Jackson." Heartbroken and homesick, she would shorten her tour, going to Charleston, Richmond, and then Martinsburg.

Belle's one-day visit to Charleston, South Carolina, began with a sightseeing tour of the city. She went on board two gunboats in the harbor and, with the aid of field glasses, viewed the ships of the Northern blockade.

That evening she dined on shore with General Pierre G. T. Beauregard and several officers of his staff. She was absolutely thrilled at the opportunity of meeting "Old Bory." This general of French ancestry had a remarkable military career. He demanded and received the surrender of Fort Sumter at the beginning of the war; he was then charged with the defense of the South Carolina coast. He was later shifted to Virginia and his command merged with that of General Robert E. Lee. He is described as "a small man of typically French appearance, soldierly in bearing, animated and agreeable in manner."[5]

After dinner, one officer presented her with a large supply of fresh fruit, part of the cargo of a blockade runner which had just arrived from Nassau. In addition to the oranges, pineapples, and bananas, the officer gave her a handsome parrot which she managed to take to her next stop, Richmond.

One result of her Charleston visit was her recognition of the effectiveness of the naval blockade proclaimed by Lincoln. It was the chief strategic device used by the North to ultimately defeat the South.[6] The Confederacy's survival depended on exports of cotton, grain, and other agricultural products, and imports of guns, ammunition, medicine, and other supplies. The Union plan was to cut off all South Atlantic and Gulf ports from foreign commerce. If the blockade succeeded, the Confederacy could be subdued with little bloodshed.

The South experimented with new ships to break the blockade, among them the iron-clad *Merrimack* which the Yankees scuttled after its clash with the *Monitor* in Norfolk harbor when Virginia seceded. Another device tried was a torpedo boat; still another was a small cigar-shaped submarine. Such a vessel sank a ship in Charleston harbor in 1864. However, such efforts failed to break or even weaken the blockade. The Confederates then decided to prey upon the Northern merchant marine on the high seas in the hope that the Union would detach ships from the blockade, but the scheme failed and the blockade continued.[7]

The blockade, of course, gave rise to blockade runners, who had to function as spies, messengers, purchasing agents, and smugglers. Their mission was dangerous and exciting and inevitably appealed to Belle.

She left Charleston for Richmond, paying a brief visit there. Martinsburg beckoned but it was again in Union hands. When the news arrived that the Confederate troops were advancing northward toward Winchester, she was overjoyed and decided to follow at the rear of the army.

Harry Gilmor had just set out for Winchester on a scouting expedition for General Richard S. Ewell when, at Woodstock, Virginia, he met Belle who begged to accompany him. Gilmor stalled, saying that she must first get permission from his supervisor, General Jenkins, commander of the Valley District, who was paving the way for Ewell's advance. Belle remained in Woodstock to see Jenkins the next day and Gilmor thought that he could leave early next morning without her.

Gilmor arose before sunrise to discover both his saber and his pistols missing. As he frantically searched for them, Belle approached, dressed in a neat-fitting riding habit, with a pretty little belt around her waist, from which the butts of two small pistols peeped, cased in a leather holster. The pistols were Belle's insurance that she would not be left behind by early-bird Gilmor!

Gilmor later wrote,

> She rode with me to the quarters of General Jenkins, to
> whom I had to report before passing through his lines. We
> found him sitting before his tent, and after dispatching my
> business Miss Belle presented her request. I fixed myself
> rather behind her, that I might give a signal to the general not
> to consent. The fact is, I did not care to be accompanied by a
> woman on so perilous an enterprise; for, though she was a
> splendid and reckless rider, of unflinching courage, and her
> whole soul bound up in the Southern cause, yet she was a
> little—mark you only a *little*—headstrong and wilful, and I
> thought it best, both for her sake and mine, that she should
> not go. I hope Miss Belle will forgive this little ruse. The
> general, of course, refused, which made her furious, but he
> was firm, and I rode off without her.[8]

On 14 June 1863 the attack on Winchester began with Belle only
four miles from the action. The familiar sound of battle reminded her of
Front Royal and the role she played there. Deciding to at least witness
the spectacle, if not participate, she joined a wounded officer who was
too disabled to fight and rode with him to a hill from which they could
view the combat.[9] Others soon joined them, men and women on
half-starved mules and horses that had been overlooked by the
retreating enemy. Within character, Belle was riding a beautiful—and
conspicuous—white horse which soon attracted enemy gunfire!

Belle enjoyed the afternoon more than anything in months and
was now in a hurry to return home. The victorious Confederates, led
by General Lee, followed the fleeing Yankees all the way to the
Potomac.[10]

A "Lieutenant C" of Gilmor's command later observed:

> Well, there isn't a Southerner who would not lay down his life
> for her [Belle]. When I was at the battle of Winchester, I was
> wounded and she came into the hospital where I was and
> inquired if there were any Maryland boys there. Amongst
> other delicacies, she gave me some nice peach-brandy. She
> and Mrs. G. were in the fort, if I err not, cheering us on when
> we made a charge and drove the Yankees back.[11]

The Southern troops succeeded in recapturing both Winchester and Martinsburg, so Belle returned home. Her father, whose health had been broken by the hardships of the campaign, was home on leave. She had the pleasure of being welcomed by both parents, of being with her family again in her own home after such a long absence. Her sister and brothers had grown considerably and her mother was again pregnant. Belle, at least for a while, would be content to remain at home with her family.[12]

Double Jeopardy

MAY—LATE SUMMER 1863

*. . . you are a rebel, and will do more harm
to our cause* [the Union] *than half the men could do.*[1]

DURING THE MONTHS when Belle was in prison, in Knoxville, and
traveling through the deep South, several major events occurred that
would vastly affect her life and the Confederacy. The first was that her
beloved Virginia was divided, and West Virginia, which included her
home town of Martinsburg, became a separate state, joining the Union
side. Another was Robert E. Lee's retreat across the Potomac after
the Battle of Gettysburg.

Why had Virginia split in two? The tidewater region, middle
Virginia, the Piedmont, and the Shenandoah Valley were the slave-
holding areas, looking to the seaboard and the South for leadership.
The mountain areas of northwestern Virginia and the Ohio Valley
region, where slaves were few, resented the political domination of the
South. These areas felt discriminated against, opposing secession and
the organization of the Confederacy. In the eastern panhandle of West
Virginia, where Martinsburg is located, sentiment was divided. The
region was economically and geographically a part of eastern Virginia.
The Baltimore and Ohio railroad passed through the area, and Martinsburg, the main terminal, had to remain in Union hands at all cost.[2]

Steps were taken to organize a new state as early as 1861. A
convention assembled at Wheeling, in West Virginia's northern panhandle, and adopted resolutions denouncing secession. Later a "Un-

ionist government" for Virginia was put into operation at Wheeling, drawing up a constitution for a new state to be called West Virginia. The voters of the region ratified the constitution and the "restored legislature" at Wheeling, acting for all of Virginia, gave its consent to the formation of the new state. Congress in Washington passed legislation admitting the new state to the Union and President Lincoln proclaimed West Virginia admitted, effective 20 June 1863.[3]

The eastern panhandle of the new state found this development hard to accept. They doubted the constitutionality of the action. To this day, older residents of the panhandle call West Virginia the "bastard state of a political rape." Sentiment was more divided than ever; families were torn apart, brothers fought on opposite sides, and Belle was now a "woman without a home," since Martinsburg was a part of the Union. Forbidden to cross Confederate lines, she legally could not go home again, but the restriction only made her defiant and determined to remain in Martinsburg.

On the military front General Robert E. Lee had made another effort to carry the war into Union territory. By way of the Shenandoah Valley he moved rapidly through Maryland and Pennsylvania, confronting the Union army at Gettysburg. The attack came on 1 July and continued for two more days without obvious advantage to either side. On the afternoon of 3 July Lee sent fresh troops into action under the command of General George E. Pickett—the famous "Pickett's charge." Pickett lost two-thirds of his troops, ending the heaviest fighting of the Battle of Gettysburg.[4]

The hopes of the South were blighted in this battle which most historians consider the turning point of the war.[5] On the evening of 4 July, Lee retreated to the Potomac River, having lost a third of his army, camping for a few days on the Maryland side because of high water from heavy rains. Lee then retreated across the Potomac, returning by way of the new West Virginia, to Virginia.[6]

Meanwhile, yet another disaster to the South occurred at Vicksburg on the Mississippi River. On that same 4 July, Union General U. S. Grant captured Vicksburg, opening up the whole Mississippi valley to Union control. The fall of Vicksburg, coming the day after the loss of Gettysburg, was doubly shattering to Confederate morale.[7]

Before the end of the year a third turning point of the war was reached—this one in Tennessee. The Union Army under General

William S. Rosecrans occupied Chattanooga (9 September). He then pursued General Braxton Bragg, leader of the Confederate Army, across the Georgia line. They clashed in the Battle of Chickamauga (19-20 September). This was one of the few battles where the Confederates had a numerical superiority (70,000 vs. 56,000). Part of the Union army retreated, but the remainder, under General George H. Thomas ("the Rock of Chickamauga"), continued to fight. Finally General U. S. Grant came to the rescue and the Union army drove the Confederates off Missionary Ridge and Lookout Mountain (this was the "Battle Above the Clouds") and back into Georgia. Union troops then occupied most of Tennessee, having achieved another important objective—control of the Tennessee River. They had split the Confederacy again. The only hope of the defeated Southerners was to win by holding on and exhausting the Northern will to fight.[8]

After Gettysburg, Martinsburg became one continuous hospital. All available buildings were used—churches, schools, and private homes, including Belle's. The railroad facilities had been burned and roads were in poor shape. Martinsburg was economically stagnant, with business almost entirely suspended. There was great distress in the community: food, medical supplies, and clothing were in short supply. Streets and property were seriously damaged. From the beginning of the war to the end, there were camps of Union or Confederate soldiers in the town, with a change of occupants sometimes occurring several times in one day.[9]

It was during this occupation that Mrs. Boyd gave birth to a daughter. Her health was generally poor, and Belle's father's health had been badly impaired by hardships in the army. Belle decided to remain at home—even if it meant arrest and return to prison. She was going to stay.

> I had been from home so long, and my Mother and father were so anxious that I should remain with them, that I hoped, by keeping quiet, to be allowed to do so. My Mother was taken very ill just as the Confederates evacuated the town— and for a time all was quiet.[10]

But one morning Belle saw some Union troops halt in front of the house. Mr. Boyd answered the door and summoned Belle, who descended the stairs to the drawing room. She was introduced to Major Nathan Goff of the Third West Virginia Infantry.

"Miss Boyd, General Kelly commanded me to call and see if you really had remained at home, such a report having reached headquarters; but he did not credit it, so I have come to ascertain the truth."

"Major Goff, what is there so peculiarly strange in my remaining in my own home with my parents?"

"But do you not think it rather dangerous?" blurted the exasperated Goff. "Are you not afraid of being arrested?"

"Oh no! For I don't know why they should do so, I am no criminal!"

"Yes, true, but you are a rebel, and will do more harm to our cause than half the men could do."

"But there are other rebels besides myself," protested Belle.

"Yes, but then not so dangerous as yourself."[11]
After further brief conversation Major Goff withdrew, bidding Belle good morning.

Several days passed quietly and Belle dared to hope that she would not be molested. Then came the order for her arrest. Ben Boyd pleaded that Belle be allowed to stay at home during her mother's illness. Strangely enough, the request was granted: Belle was merely placed on parole, with sentries stationed around the house. Her movements were extremely limited; she was not even allowed to go out on the balcony.[12]

Mr. Boyd felt that Belle's constant care saved her mother's life. This critical period meant a great deal to both of them and they grew even closer. Noting the deep circles under his eyes, Belle realized the strain he had been under and feared for his future and her own.

The July weather was unusually warm and Belle became listless and despondent. The heat, the constant nursing of her mother, her confinement indoors, her father's continued worry, and the lack of activity combined to make her wretched. She had been under constant surveillance for over a month, prevented from leaving her home except by special pass.

On one occasion, desiring to take a walk, she secured a permit from the commanding officer. "Miss Belle Boyd has permission to walk out for half an hour, at 5 o'clock this A.M., giving her word of honor that she will use nothing which she may see or hear to the disadvantage of U.S. troops."[13]

Despite the pass, Belle had walked only a few blocks from home when she was arrested and returned home with a guard on each side, carrying loaded muskets. Within an hour she received a note from Union headquarters informing her that, although on parole, she was not allowed to promenade in Martinsburg! Apparently, the thinking at Union headquarters was that Belle was too troublesome to be allowed any freedom. Captain James H. Stevenson of the First New York (Lincoln) Cavalry, stationed in Martinsburg, was dispatched to have a chat with her:

"I hope you are not afraid of a poor weak woman," Belle observed sarcastically. "What do you hear about me?"

"Well, it is rumored that you led Stuart's column in his raid around McClellan on the Peninsula, and also a similar raid in Maryland."

"You all don't believe that, do you?" Belle laughed.

"Well, the men think so, but if you deny it I will believe you." Belle then excused herself and went upstairs, soon reappearing in the uniform of a Confederate colonel of cavalry. As Stevenson wrote later,

> She wore a fine gray cloth jacket, slashed with gold lace on the breast and sleeves, a pair of white buckskin gauntlets, a dove-colored soft felt hat, with a long dark plume, and a gray skirt or riding habit. A fine leather belt, with a silver-mounted revolver in a patent-leather case, ornamented her waist, and she carried a fancy riding whip in her hand. She was tall and of good figure and, in her uniform looked well. She wore the rank of a colonel C.S.A. and she told me she often rode with General Stuart at the head of his cavalry. She showed me a gold watch, studded with jewels, presented to her by the officers of Stuart's cavalry, as the inscription proved. Altogether she seemed very proud of her connection with the Confederate raiders, and of the services she had rendered to the Confederacy.[14]

Stevenson feigned alarm, told her he would surrender, begged her not to shoot—at which she laughed heartily, saying that was the way Yankees acted when General Stuart met them! Stevenson then assured Belle that she would not be molested as long as she remained in the house. Sentinels would remain stationed around the premises to keep her from communicating with anyone.

Lunsford Lindsay Lomax of the 11th Virginia Cavalry was one of Stuart's brigade commanders and may have been one of the officers who presented Belle with the watch she showed Stevenson. In 1944 Lomax's daughter, Mrs. Lindsay Lomax Wood, wrote:

> From childhood the story of Belle Boyd thrilled me. For a time she was my Father's spy and he delighted in telling me of her reckless bravery for the Confederacy. I only regret that with the passage of time I've forgotten many of the romantic stories he told me. . . .
>
> My Father gave me the impression that she was fearless, but never haphazard in her endeavors to help the Confederacy. I may be wrong, but I think it was somewhere near Winchester when she did some scouting duty for him.[15]

Another month passed and Belle was in constant suspense. What would be her fate? At last, when all were hoping that she would soon be free, Provost Marshal Major Walker called, accompanied by a detective. She must prepare to return to Washington, they told her, by order of Secretary of War Stanton, at eleven o'clock the following morning.

Belle was stymied: there was no hope of escape as the house was vigilantly guarded. Her mother, gradually recovering, weakened again at the thought of Belle being imprisoned once more. Ben Boyd was determined that the nineteen-year-old girl should not go unaccompanied; besides, he might be able to hasten negotiations and bring her back to Martinsburg. So, the next morning, Ben left with Belle for Washington.[16]

CHAPTER NINETEEN

Carroll Prison

LATE SUMMER—DECEMBER 1863

*Once more iron bars shut me off from the outer world,
and from all that is dear in this life.*[1]

IN THE LATE SUMMER of 1863 Belle arrived at Carroll Prison which adjoined the Old Capitol Prison. The large brick building was a former hotel belonging to Duff Green, a newspaper editor, friend of Andrew Jackson's, and a member of his "kitchen cabinet." Belle glumly viewed the prison; she had never been inside it, but knew well its reputation for dirt and disease. Sometimes called the "Yankee Bastille," it had been converted into a pen for rebels, political prisoners, blockade runners, prisoners of state, smugglers, spies, criminals, and Federal officers convicted of defrauding the government.[2]

Belle's father had been a great comfort to her on the train from Martinsburg. Now he sat opposite her in the carriage on the ride from the railroad station to the prison, holding her hand in both of his. He probably intended to use what influence he possessed to get her released. Unknown to both of them, their tender farewell at the prison gate would be their last.

The familiar figure of Superintendent Wood greeted Belle. Supervisor of both the Old Capitol and Carroll prisons, Wood's mocking voice had not changed, nor his peculiar kind of kindness. He instructed a guard to take her to the "room for distinguished guests," but her cell had the smell of sweat and filth. The heat almost overcame her; how cool it had seemed outside! Her room was supposed to be the "nicest" in the place, except for some offices attached to the building.

It was the Old Capitol all over again: dirty walls with broken plaster, meager furniture (a bed, chair, and dresser) and a single barred window. A sentry appeared with her noon meal of bread, meat, and potatoes. At one point, a jangling sound diverted her; it was Mr. Lockwood, the appropriately surnamed keeper of the keys. He was always "prying about" when not otherwise engaged, noted Belle.[3]

"Once more iron bars shut me off from the outside world and from all that is dear in this life," wrote Belle sadly as she spent most of the first day near the window. "Again my monotonous prison routine began."[4] Was this to be her life for months to come? She slept fitfully that first night. The second day was like the first. She had made many friends in the Old Capitol Prison next door; would the inmates of Carroll Prison be as congenial?

She especially remembered Dennis Mahony, the newspaper editor from Iowa, and Joseph Kerbey, the Boy Spy from Pennsylvania; Gus Williams, the one who sang so well; and General Doster and J. J. Williamson who were later to write about their prison experiences.

Perhaps her thoughts turned to Clifford McVay and their brief romance. She could see him across the hall, eyeing her, waiting for her to return his message. What had become of him? Was he still alive and in the Old Capitol next door? Did he return to his regiment? Would she ever see him again? Belle was lonely, homesick, and sorry for herself.

> It seemed to me that the world would never go round on its axis; for the days and nights were interminably long, and many, many were the hours that I spent gazing forth through the bars of my grated windows with an apathetic listlessness. Yet there were times when I wished that my soul were but free to soar away from those who held me captive.[5]

A few days after her arrival she heard the familiar sound of an instrument grating the wall. The plaster gave way and a knife blade peeped through. She set to work on her side and soon there was a hole large enough for passing tightly-rolled notes. Her neighbors turned out to be gentlemen named Brookes, Warren, Stuart, and Williams. They had been there for nine months, charged with attempting to go South and enlist in the Confederate Army.

This communication lasted but briefly, for Mr. Lockwood discovered the hole, moved the gentlemen to another room, and repaired the opening. Belle had at first seen Lockwood as a possible friend, but she now suspected him of spying on the inmates.

Several days later Belle learned that she was to have a companion, Miss Ida P., arrested on the charge of being a rebel mail-carrier. Belle was allowed to speak to the new inmate when she arrived and soon learned that Ida was to occupy the room vacated by her former communicants. Belle watched as the door between the rooms was boarded over, noting which plank covered the keyhole.

How to remove the plank? It did not yield to bare hands. Belle resorted to what she did best: she offered their sentinel some apples and oranges, talked and joked with him, and then asked him to lend her his bayonet. He paused for an instant, then unfixed it from his gun. With a twinkle in his eye he whispered, "Be quick, Miss," and disappeared down the hall.

Belle was in the midst of wrenching the board from the door when Superintendent Wood came up the stairway. She thrust the bayonet under the bed just as Wood entered the room. "If you'd like to chat with me and Miss Ida, her room is larger," Belle offered. The bluff worked and they joined Ida next door.

After remaining there a few minutes, Belle begged leave to get a handkerchief. She ran to her room, tore off the board with the bayonet, and returned the weapon to the sentry. As she returned, Wood was boasting that "There warn't anything going on in that prison that he didn't know of."[6]

Although Belle succeeded in creating a passageway for communication, a few days later, Ida P., having sworn that she would do nothing more against the Union government, was released.

A young English journalist, George Lawrence, came to America to gather material for articles for the *London Morning Post*. Unwilling to see the war from the Northern lines only, or to accept uncritically the Federal attitude toward the issues, he journeyed from one side to the other. However, his journalistic objectivity began to fail, and he grew increasingly sympathetic with the South, ultimately trying to join the Confederate Army. He found himself a fellow-prisoner with Belle Boyd.[7]

One day, as he walked in the courtyard, he noticed a beautiful woman behind the bars of a second-story window.

> I saw a figure in the freshest summer toilette of cool pink muslin; close braids of dark hair shading clear pale cheeks; eyes that were made to sparkle, tho the look in them was very sad, and the languid bowing down of the small head told of something worse than weariness. Truly a pretty picture, tho framed in such a rude setting.

Lawrence later learned that he had been admiring Belle Boyd. On another occasion:

> One evening I chanced to be loitering almost under the window; a low significant cough made me look up, I saw the flash of a gold bracelet, the wave of a white hand; and there fell at my feet a fragrant pearly rosebud, nestling in fresh green leaves.[8]

Carroll Prison was much like the Old Capitol, or perhaps Belle's presence made it so. In time, she and the other prisoners came to communicate and know one another and she found sympathetic sentinels and townspeople in the street below. Belle still loved to sing the Southern songs and the other prisoners would join in the chorus, their voices resounding inside and outside the prison walls.[9]

One evening, Belle sat at her window, singing "Take Me Back To My Sunny South." A crowd on the opposite side of the street listened awhile, then departed. As Belle sat by the window a while longer, something whizzed by her head and struck the opposite wall. She almost screamed at an imagined assassination attempt, but to her astonishment saw an arrow quivering in the opposite wall, a letter fastened to it.

> Poor girl! You have the deepest sympathy of all the best community in Washington City, and there are many who would lay down their lives for you, but they are powerless to act or aid you at present. *You have many very warm friends*; and we daily watch the journals to see if there is any news of you. If you will listen attentively to the instructions that I give you, you will be able to correspond with and hear from your friends outside.

The letter included instructions for placing a letter in a cut-open India rubber ball, then sewing the ball together again. She was to throw the ball out her window, with as much force as she could exert, across the street and into the square. Someone would be there at certain times to retrieve the ball. The letter ended, "Trust me, I will get it. *Do not be afraid. I am really your friend. C. H.*"[10]

Belle hesitated, doubting the propriety or safety of replying—it might be a trick. But prudence yielded to the delight of having an unknown friend and thus began a correspondence that continued for the remainder of her time in prison. Through C. H. she acquired news of the outside world and received small Confederate flags made by the ladies of Washington.

The prison guards suspected that Belle was sending and receiving information, both inside and outside the prison, but she outwitted and tormented them, never getting caught in the act. Some of the guards considered this communication a game played by the inmates.

To Belle, the monotony of prison life was almost unbearable. One diversion she devised was to fasten a Confederate flag to a broom handle and suspend it outside her window. When it was discovered by a guard, he would angrily enter the room and seize the flag. Sometimes a musket shot would be aimed at her window, hitting her ceiling or wall with a heavy thud. Belle, giving the sentinel no time to reload, would tauntingly appear at the window as if nothing had happened.

Despite these diversions, Belle became listless and depressed, losing her appetite, spending sleepless nights. Her health declined. Summer heat, close confinement, and lack of exercise took their toll and she succumbed to typhoid fever. Growing worse under the care of a Federal physician, she did not begin to recover until attended by a fellow-prisoner, a Confederate surgeon who voluntarily assumed her care.[11]

In her depressed state she became the victim of self-pity—she was away from home, there were no close friends near, no one to care for and comfort her "save an humble negress, who nursed me through my illness as though she had been my own 'black mammee' "; no communication with her family, and no real desire to recover. Secretary of War Stanton refused to release her. Finally, after three weeks under the treatment of the friendly physician, she began to improve; at the end of the fourth week, she began to walk again.

As her energy returned, so did her belligerence toward the Federal government. She wrote a note to President Lincoln and its flippancy may explain why she does not mention it in her own book (although the actual note survives today in the Brown University

> Carroll Prison
> Washington, D.C.
> September 17th, 1863.
> To his Excellency
> The President of the U.S.,

Mr. Lincoln—
Tis for the purpose of begging that you will honor me with a call that I write you.

> Yours very respectfully,
> Belle Boyd[12]

As Belle recuperated, a prison official stopped in to tell her that a "beautiful woman" had arrived. She was in a room at the end of the hall on the floor below her. A day or so later Belle met this "beautiful woman" in the hall and they stared at each other in amazement. To the prison official the new arrival was "beautiful," but to Belle she was only Annie Jones, the woman she had befriended in Front Royal and who had repaid Belle's kindness by denouncing her to the Federals, causing her arrest! Belle scorned her, but later pitied this woman, a reputed camp follower (prostitute), who was transferred from prison to an insane asylum.[13]

Throughout Belle's captivity official proceedings against her were conducted under Major Levi C. Turner, an investigator from the Judge Advocate's department. Belle characterized these proceedings as a trial by court-martial. When she learned that she was to be sentenced to hard labor at the Fitchburg, Massachusetts jail for the duration of the war, Belle suffered a relapse of the fever from which she had just recovered. Belle's father, who was in Martinsburg when he heard of the sentence and her second illness, immediately came to Washington to exert his influence in her behalf. After his untiring exertions, and those of friends, the sentence was modified to "Banishment to the South—never to return North again during the war."[14]

Ben Boyd probably appealed to his old friend and fellow West Virginian, Ward Hill Lamon, currently Marshal of the District of

Columbia, and a lifelong friend of Lincoln's.[15] There is a persistent legend that Belle was sentenced to die but that humanitarian President Lincoln changed the sentence to less severe punishment. There is no hard evidence of the truth of the story. Since Belle was a special prisoner of the War Department, only the President or Secretary of War could have commuted the sentence. History does prove that Lincoln was susceptible to requests of clemency and Stanton was not always successful in preventing such presidential action.[16]

When Belle recovered her energy, she was allowed to walk thirty minutes each day in the prison yard, but not to communicate, orally or in writing, with anyone. She was to be followed by a corporal and a guard carrying muskets. Belle, of course, did not take such rules very seriously. On one occasion, a party of young girls passed and dropped at her feet a piece of bristol board bearing a flag and her name, worked upon it in worsted. The corporal grabbed the gift and commanded the whole group to halt immediately. But for the entreaties of Belle and the girls themselves, he would have arrested them. As it happened, he proved merciful and dismissed them. Belle gave him five dollars, promising never to say anything to implicate him.[17]

Belle's walks drew so much attention from the curious and the sympathizers that Stanton revoked the privilege, confining her to her room. "Thus my promenade became one of the things of the past."[18]

Belle always seemed to have money. Wood reported that Belle's father sent her, from time to time, large sums, most of which was spent for the comfort of the other prisoners and to aid in obtaining their release.[19] Some was smuggled in, given by friends outside. When it was learned that she was soon to leave the prison, other things were secretly sent, including army supplies, gauntlets, and clothing. She packed them in her trunk, locked it, and kept the key on her person. In that way she was able to take them with her when she departed.[20]

Before Belle left for the South, one of the imprisoned Confederate officers gave her letters of introduction to the vice-president of the Confederacy, Alexander Hamilton Stephens, and to Bowling Baker, Chief Auditor of the Southern Treasury Department. Both letters stressed her untiring devotion to the Confederacy, the zeal that she had shown to serve her country at all times, and her kindness to her fellow-prisoners. The letters were contraband, but Belle thought she would be able to smuggle them out.[21]

One evening, as she looked out her room door, she heard a significant cough, followed by a tightly rolled note thrown towards her. A Mr. K. of Virginia was begging her to aid him and two friends in escaping. Jeopardizing her own release, slated for the first of December, she promised to help and gave him forty dollars. By means of her rubber ball, arrangements were made and the night of escape was fixed.

As the escape time approached, Belle grew fearful, for she had much to lose, but she went ahead as planned. Asking to see Superintendent Wood on business, Belle managed to detain him with interesting conversation. Suddenly, from the corner of the prison that faced the street, came a cry of "Murder! Murder!" It was part of the escape strategy and it worked perfectly: at the first cry, Wood rushed to the scene, and was quickly joined by some soldiers who were loitering outside.

Meanwhile the escaping prisoners left through the roof, scrambled out upon the eaves, descended by means of a lightning conductor to the street below, and made their getaway, later arriving safely in Richmond. There were tense moments at Carroll Prison, for Belle was suspected of having a part in the conspiracy, knowing more than she pretended about the affair. However, the investigation could prove nothing against her and she was not punished.[22]

Belle's last days at Carroll Prison were rather peaceful. She had the goodwill of the inmates and of Superintendent Wood. The Northern press had printed very little about her. Perhaps the press (or the War Department) considered publicity undesirable because of the public interest aroused by her earlier imprisonment. Perhaps the U. S. government considered her less dangerous and less influential if she were not in Washington, but in the South, where of course her press notices were much better:

> Had I been a queen, or a reigning princess, my every movement could not have been more faithfully chronicled at this period of my imprisonment. My health was bulletined for the gratification of the public; and if I walked or was indisposed, it was announced after the most approved fashion by the newspapers. Thus, from the force of circumstances, and not through any desire of my own, I became a celebrity.[23]

CHAPTER TWENTY

Beauty and the Beast

1-5 DECEMBER 1863

*I must acknowledge that I do feel frightened
in the presence of a man of such world-wide
reputation as yourself.*[1]

EARLY ON THE MORNING of 1 December 1863, Belle left Carroll Prison for Fortress Monroe. Her escort was Captain James Mix, a former bodyguard for President Lincoln, indicating her importance as a "prisoner of state." Belle's father had hoped to accompany her, but just before her departure came the distressing news that he was too ill to travel. He remained at the home of his niece in Washington.[2] Union officials denied her pleas to see him.[3]

Belle arrived at Fortress Monroe early the following morning. From there she was to take an exchange boat to Richmond, but not immediately, for the boat was not then ready. In the meantime, she would be a charge of General Benjamin "Beast" Butler, one of the most dreaded leaders of the Union Army.[4]

During Butler's occupation of New Orleans earlier in the war, he showed himself to be arrogant, merciless, corrupt, and utterly without compassion. He was best known for his infamous Order Number 28, which provided that "When any female shall, by word, gesture, or movement, insult or show contempt for any officer or soldier of the USA, she shall be regarded and held liable to be treated as a woman of the town plying her avocation."[5]

The South's regard for General Butler was nicely put in this acrostic, published in the Charleston *Daily Courier* on 9 February 1863:

Brutal and vulgar, a coward and knave;
Famed for no action, noble or brave;
Beastly by instinct, a drunkard and sot;
Ugly and venomous, on mankind a blot;
Thief, liar, and scoundrel in highest degree;
Let Yankeedom boast of such heroes as thee;
Every woman and child shall for ages to come,
Remember thee, monster, thou vilest of scum.[6]

Even England was aroused by Order Number 28. Prime Minister Lord Palmerston said, "Any Englishman must blush to think that such an act has been committed by one belonging to the Anglo-Saxon race."[7] When Butler was criticized by the House of Parliament, he pointed out that he had merely borrowed his proclamation from the Ordinances of London.[8]

About November 1863, General Butler had assumed command of Virginia and North Carolina, making his headquarters at Fortress Monroe.[9] Edward Pollard, editor of the *Richmond Examiner*, described him as "a man with a large head which gave one the idea of a bulky and unwieldy figure. . . . He talks with a perpetual motion of his features."[10] One writer of the time described Butler as a "hideous, cross-eyed beast."[11]

Belle was escorted from the boat into the Fortress and then to Butler's office. As she entered, they scrutinized one another, Belle noting his shortness, balding head, drooping eyelids, and harsh mouth. Butler appraised her with curiosity and contempt.[12]

"Ah, so this is Miss Boyd, the famous Rebel Spy. Pray be seated."

"Thank you, General Butler, but I prefer to stand."

He noticed her trembling. "Pray, be seated. But why do you tremble so? Are you frightened?"

"No; ah! that is, yes, General Butler; I must acknowledge that I do feel frightened in the presence of a man of such world-wide reputation as yourself."

This seemed to please him. Rubbing his hands together and smiling, he said again. "Oh, pray do be seated, Miss Boyd." Then he added, "But what do you mean when you say that I am widely known?"

"I mean, General Butler, that you are a man whose atrocious conduct and brutality, especially to Southern ladies, is so infamous that even the English Parliament commented upon it. I naturally feel alarmed at being in your presence."[13]

Butler was quite surprised and very offended. He had expected some graceful compliment from Belle. He angrily ordered her out of his office. Belle felt very uneasy, fearing that General Butler might retaliate. He might succumb to pettiness and revenge and she pictured herself again in a prison cell.

Belle was then taken to a Norfolk hotel and required to give her word not to leave until called for. In the hotel she met Euphemia Mary Goldsborough of Baltimore and Julia and Ann Lomax, sisters of the Confederate General Lomax.[14]

Euphemia Goldsborough had a spirit kindred to Belle's. She was a Confederate courier, had tended wounded after the battles of Antietam and Gettysburg, and was considered a Rebel spy. She, too, had been sentenced to banishment.

The order came that evening for Euphemia and Belle to leave for Richmond. The Lomax sisters, suspected of spying, were not allowed to proceed, but were returned to Baltimore.

When the time came for departure, Euphemia and Belle were taken to the office of the Provost Marshal. There Belle found her luggage, two Saratoga trunks and a bonnet box. She surrendered her keys to some inspectors (a man and two women) who thoroughly examined the contents of her baggage. Belle assured them that they need not search her luggage as she had just come from prison, and that they would find nothing of interest, but her appeal was ignored.

The inspectors were astonished and Belle was embarrassed when they pulled from the bottom of one of her trunks two suits of civilian clothes, a uniform for Major George W. _____, and a dozen linen shirts. They pulled out the army supplies which had been smuggled into Carroll prison. Close questioning followed as to how she obtained the articles, but she evaded them with vague answers. Other contraband was discovered: army gauntlets, felt hats, clothing, and a pair of field glasses which had belonged to General Jackson. She begged to keep the field glasses, but to her mortification, they were given to General Butler.

The worst was yet to come: a personal search! She had concealed in her clothing $20,000 in Confederate notes, $5,000 in greenbacks, and nearly $1,000 in gold. Letters of introduction from her friends in Carroll Prison were also secreted on her person. She argued, passionately and pitifully, pleading for them not to disgrace her with the indignity of a personal search. As it grew late, one of her antagonists wearily allowed, "Well, if you will take an oath to the effect that you have nothing contraband upon you—no letters or papers—you shall not be searched."

Belle realized that she must concede a bit in order to win, so she volunteered that she did have, well, a couple of letters. He asked if she had money. Well, yes, some Confederate money; but he sneeringly informed her that she could keep "that stuff." He then opened the letters and grew angry as he saw the remarks about her "services to my country" and her "devotion to the Southern cause." Angrily he said, "I shall send this to General Butler in the morning. I would do so now, but it is after office hours."[15]

Euphemia, who had been searched earlier that morning, was a quiet spectator to the affair. Her reaction to the search and questioning is not mentioned by Belle; however, Euphemia also kept a diary. Referring to the Fortress Monroe episode in an item dated 4 December 1863, she says: "I forgot to say that horrid woman, Belle Boyd, was sent up on the same truce boat with me, but enough of her."[16] (There is no indication of why Euphemia found Belle "horrid.").

Belle and Euphemia were then taken to the wharf, placed on board a tug, and sent to the exchange boat, the *City of New York*. They were kindly received aboard by Major Mulford and his wife, who showed them to their quarters. The boat remained at anchor all night and sailed for Richmond the following morning.

Shortly after they departed, Belle noticed a boat following them; it was the steam tug that had brought them to the *City of New York*. Belle was alarmed, fearing pursuit; perhaps General Butler, angry over the letters, had ordered her detained. However, the *City of New York* had already waited so long that Major Mulford ordered "full steam ahead."[17]

Belle afterwards learned that her fears were not unfounded. When General Butler, angry at Belle's insolence, had read the letters taken from her, he ordered her followed and captured and sent to Fort Warren on Massachusetts Bay. As Butler issued this order he remarked to those around him that he would play the leading character in "Beauty and the Beast." When the tug returned from the fruitless chase he was extremely angry, frustrated, and exasperated. Belle notes: "This I had from such good authority that I am confident the General will not feel it worth his while to contradict the statement."[18]

Child of the Confederacy

5 DECEMBER 1863—28 MARCH 1864

*I had always been termed
the "Child of the Confederacy."*[1]

T HE *CITY OF NEW YORK* met the Federal blockading fleet at the mouth of the James River and was stopped for an inspection. They then sailed up the river and Belle was again alive, home in her beloved Southland, free to breathe the Virginia air. They arrived in Richmond around eight o'clock on a beautiful moonlit night. Belle went immediately to a prominent Richmond hotel, the Spotswood House, where, fatigued from her journey, she retired.

When I came down to breakfast on the following day, my many acquaintances and friends in the hotel were astonished to see me, for few had expected that I should be released, and none that I should so soon arrive at Richmond. The morning papers announced my return in flattering terms . . . but, alas! my happiness was of short duration, and my freedom was dearly bought. . . .

On Monday morning, the 14th, before I had risen, I received a little note from Captain Hatch, in which he expressed great sorrow at having to be the bearer of mournful tidings, and said that, as soon as I was dressed, he would call in person with the wife of the proprietor of the hotel. For one moment I could not imagine what he meant, but, dressing myself as speedily as I possibly could, I sent for them.

They came: Captain Hatch held in his hands a newspaper. He approached me, saying,

"Miss Belle, you are aware that you left your father ill?"

In one moment I comprehended every thing, and exclaiming "My God! is he dead?" I sank fainting to the floor.

This swoon was succeeded by a severe illness; and I felt all the loneliness of my position. An exile (for the Yankees held possession of Martinsburg) and an orphan—these words described me; and, ah! how hard they seemed!

One of those strange warnings that are sometimes given to mortals, or that are, some would say, the imaginings of an excited brain shaken by sickness, ought to have prepared me for my sad bereavement.

"Some say that gleams of a remoter world
Visit the soul in sleep."

The night upon which my father died I had retired to rest somewhat earlier than usual. How long I slept I do not know, but I suddenly awoke, or seemed to awaken, from my sleep, although I had neither the power nor the wish to move. In the centre of the room I saw General Jackson, whose eyes rested sorrowfully upon me. Beside him stood my father, gazing at me, but saying nothing. I was dumb, or I should have spoken, for I did not feel alarmed. As I looked upon those two standing together, General Jackson turned and spoke to my father. I remember the words distinctly.

"It is time for us to go," he said; and, taking my father's hand, he led him away, adding as he did so, "Poor child!"

I afterwards learnt by a letter from my mother . . . that my beloved father, at the news of my being South, where I should have to battle alone with the world, had grown rapidly worse, and had expired the very next day after my arrival in Richmond. My mother and the children had been sent for, and reached my father just before he died. Although he retained his senses up to the last, he frequently spoke of me, declared that I was hovering around his couch, and would become quite restless if people in the room went to a certain spot near the bed, exclaiming that "I was being torn from him!"[2]

Belle's father died on the very next day after her arrival in Richmond, 6 December 1863, at the age of forty-seven. He was buried in Green Hill Cemetery in Martinsburg.[3]

In spite of Belle's weakness and her sentence of banishment, she felt that she must join her mother at once in Martinsburg. Several Southern senators and some influential officers in charge of the exchange of prisoners wrote to the Federal government, urging that Belle be given permission to return to her widowed mother. Belle herself wrote to President Lincoln and Secretary Stanton, appealing to them as a Mason's daughter, but received no response.[4]

These letters have evidently been lost. However, the following letter to Ward Hill Lamon, a friend of both Belle and Lincoln, speaks for itself:

> Spotswood Hotel
> Richmond Va
> Dec 18th/63

Col Ward H Lamon,

Dear Sir,

To you I feel I have the right to apply (under the existing circumstances) I feel you will do all in your power to aid me. *You know* full well all regarding my arrest, imprisonment, & release. Since I have been sent South, my Father has died. Tis for the purpose of begging you will use your influence with Mr. *Lincoln* & Mr. Stanton, that I write. I have written to both of them regarding my case. I wish a Parole to be allowed to return to my Mother & remain there. You knew my Father, my Mother, & you know me. For god's sake use your influence (for I know you have it) with Mr. Lincoln, for me to return to ma. I know she is nearly broken hearted. Relieve my grief. My father dead. My Mother, nearly wild with grief & I an *exile*. Oh, God! 'tis too hard. I pray you will listen to my entreaties. Anser [sic] soon.

> Respectfully Yours
> Belle Boyd[5]

My letters to and from my mother in Martinsburg were intercepted; and from December the 16th . . . and then not until the following October, did I receive one line from her, though she had written repeatedly.

My health was very bad and my constitution greatly undermined; so in February I went from Richmond farther south, visiting Mobile, Atlanta, Augusta, and other cities. . . .

I cannot express one-half the gratitude that I feel to the many kind hosts whom I met in my journey through the South. During my illness in Richmond I was well cared for; and amongst the warmest of my friends must be ranked the wife of the world-renowned Captain Semmes, afterwards Admiral Semmes, of the ill-fated *Alabama*.[6]

(Admiral Semmes's ship *Alabama* was the most successful raider in the Confederacy. After the war, it was credited with having destroyed fifty-eight vessels worth $6,547,000.)[7]

Mrs. Semmes treated me with as much attention as though I had been her own daughter, and invited me to visit them at their home in Mobile. I had always been termed "the child of the Confederacy," or "the child of the army" and, no matter where I went, I was welcomed both by the gentry and the people.

In March I returned to Richmond, when, although somewhat recovered, my health still required care. I could not return home, and I felt, moreover, restless and unhappy at the death of my father. I determined, therefore, to visit Europe so soon as I could arrange my affairs. When I made known this resolution to President Davis, he approved of the plan, considering me to need quiet and rest in some place remote from the dangers of our sorely-pressed country.[8]

But Belle being Belle, it would not end there. Her imagination began to churn. Why not carry dispatches to Europe? Why not represent the Confederate States of America in European capitals? True, she had never been to Europe, but she could go to England first, and, at least, she spoke their language. She could conceal her identity on board ship by traveling under an assumed name. Her ill health and need for recuperation could be an excuse. She could pose as a private person traveling for personal reasons.

Evidently, President Davis liked the notion:

> Orders were given to the Confederate Secretary of State to make me the bearer of dispatches. I commenced preparations for departure as speedily as possible. . . .[9]

And a receipt survives to prove her role (See illustration, 130).

Returning to Belle's narrative:

> At last, on March 29th, I was able to leave Richmond. . . .
>
> Owing to an accident on the railway, we did not arrive in Wilmington [North Carolina, popular departure point for blockade runners] until several hours after the departure of the blockade-runner in which I was to have sailed.
>
> This steamer would not be followed by another for at least a fortnight, because they did not run out during the brilliant nights of the full moon, lest they should fall an easy prey to Yankee blockaders. I was therefore obliged to await the arrival and departure of the next regular steamer. . . .[11]

A Captive

(1864)

(Note: Because Belle tells the story so well, her book is quoted extensively in the following chapters.)

Proof positive of Belle Boyd's work as a "bearer of dispatches for the Dept. of State." From Louis A. Sigaud, "More About Belle Boyd," article in the February 1948 Lincoln Herald. (Courtesy of the estate of Louis A. Sigaud.)

CHAPTER TWENTY-TWO

Capture
at Sea

29 MARCH—10 MAY 1864

It was a nightmare never to be forgotten—
a night of silent, almost breathless anxiety.[1]

W ARTIME JOURNEYS ACROSS the Atlantic were difficult and dangerous—Southern ports were blockaded and the only vessels able to get
through were the blockade runners. They carried Southern goods to
Europe and returned with desperately needed arms, medicine, and
other supplies. The blockade runners had practically no accommodations for passengers and those who traveled were usually Southern
agents on official business to connections abroad.[2]

Belle waited some ten days, exploring the city. Wilmington was
very prosperous compared to Richmond, its shops filled with expensive goods. Now she understood the stories about fantastic returns
from blockade running. In the South there was a constant demand for
manufactured goods; consequently, the successful blockade runner
could be assured of a handsome profit.[3]

One of the first vessels that arrived was the *Greyhound*,
commanded by Captain Henry, formerly, it is said, an officer
in the United States navy, and who had, at the commence-
ment of the war, with many of his comrades, sent in his
resignation to the United States Navy Department, and
entered the Confederate service. Captain "Henry" had formerly been on "Stonewall" Jackson's staff; and, as I was

acquainted with his family, I gladly accepted his kind invitation, and took passage on board the *Greyhound*, feeling
doubly secure under such a skilful commander.[4]

One of the *Greyhound's* two other passengers, the *Richmond
Examiner's* editor, Edward Pollard also described Henry:

> What a splendid fellow he was; a graceful dash of manner
> which yet beamed with intelligence, an exhuberant hospital-
> ity, a kindness. . . . He had been all over the world, was
> familiar with the great capitals of Europe; bore the marks of a
> wound obtained in the campaign of Stonewall Jackson; and
> as to his name and nationality—why, passengers on block-
> ade runners are not expected to be inquisitive of these
> circumstances. . . .[5]

(In fact, "Captain Henry" was George H. Bier, using an assumed name
in the custom of Confederate agents.[6])

The *Greyhound* was a nearly new propeller steamer, painted a
light lead gray, with three fore and aft masts, weighing 400 tons. She
was a fast sailer, as well she needed to be, and she flew the British flag.[7]

> On the 8th of May I bade farewell to many friends in
> Wilmington, and stepped on board the *Greyhound* [regis-
> tered as "Mrs. Lewis"]. It was, as may well be imagined, an
> anxious moment. I knew that the venture was a desperate
> one; but I felt sustained by the greatness of my cause. . . . I
> looked to Fortune, who is so often the handmaid of a daring
> enterprise.[8]

Belle's anxiety would have been greater had she known how
well informed the Yankees were regarding the movements of the
Greyhound. Records show frequent communication between the
U. S. consul at Liverpool and the U. S. Navy regarding the vessel.[9]

> At the mouth of the river we dropped anchor, and
> decided to wait until the already waning moon should
> entirely disappear. . . .
> About ten o'clock orders were given to get under way.
> The next minute every light was extinguished, the anchor
> was weighed, steam was got up rapidly and silently, and we
> glided off just as "the trailing garments of the night" spread
> their last folds over the ocean.

The decks were piled with bales of cotton, upon which our look-out men were stationed, straining their eyes to pierce the darkness and give timely notice of the approach of an enemy. . . . No one thought of sleep. Few words were spoken. It was a night never to be forgotten—a night of silent, almost breathless anxiety. It seemed to us as if day would never break; but it came at last, and, to our unspeakable joy, not a sail was in sight. We were moving unmolested and alone upon a tranquil sea, and we indulged in the fond hope that we had eluded our eager foes.

[Although Belle failed to note it, the dawn broke on a special day for her—May 9th—her 20th birthday.]

Steaming on, we ran close by the wreck of the Confederate iron-clad *Raleigh*, which had so lately driven the Federal blockading squadron out to sea, but which now lay on a shoal, an utter wreck, parted amidships, destroyed, not by the Federals, but by a visitation of Providence.

At this point we three passengers began to experience those sensations which, although invariably an object of derision to persons who are exempt from them, are, for the time being, as grievous to the sufferer as any in the whole catalogue of pains and aches to which flesh is heir. Reader, may it never be your lot, as it then was mine, to find sea-sickness overcome by the stronger emotion inspired by the sight of a hostile vessel bearing rapidly down with the purpose of depriving you of your freedom.

It was just noon, when a thick haze which had lain upon the water lifted, and at that moment we heard a startled cry of "Sail ho!" from the look-out man at the mast-head. These ominous words were the signal for a general rush aft. Extra steam was got up in an incredibly short space of time, and sail was set with the view both of increasing our speed and of steadying our vessel as she dashed through the water.

Alas! it was soon evident that our exertions were useless, for every minute visibly lessened the distance between us and our pursuer . . . we might look to New York instead of Bermuda as our destination.

My feelings at this intelligence must be imagined: I can describe them but inadequately. "Unless," I thought, "Providence interposes directly in our behalf, we shall be over-hauled and captured; and then what follows? I shall suffer a third rigorous imprisonment. . . ."

The chase continued, and the cruiser still gained upon us. . . . How long I remained watching I know not, but the iron messenger of death came at last. A thin, white curl of smoke rose high in the air as the enemy puffed up and presented her formidable broadside. Almost simultaneously with the hissing sound of the shell, as it buried itself in the sea within a few yards of us, came the smothered report of its explosion under water.

The enemy's shots now followed each other in rapid succession: some fell very close, while others, less skilfully aimed, were wide of the mark, and burst high in the air over our heads. During this time bale after bale of cotton had been rolled overboard by our crew, the epitaph of each, as it disappeared beneath the waves, being, "By ____! there's another they shall not get."

Our captain paced nervously to and fro, now watching the compass, now gazing fixedly at the approaching enemy, now shouting, "More steam! give her more steam!" At last he turned suddenly round to me, and exclaimed in passionate accents—

"Miss Belle, I declare to you that, but for your presence on board, I would burn her to the water's edge rather than those infernal scoundrels should reap the benefit of a single bale of our cargo."

To this I replied, "Captain H., act without reference to me—do what you think your duty. For my part, sir, I concur with you: burn her by all means—I am not afraid. I have made up my mind, and am indifferent to my fate, if only the Federals do not get the vessel."

To this Captain H. made no reply, but turned abruptly away and walked aft, where his officers were standing in a group. With them he held a hurried consultation, and then, coming to where I was seated, exclaimed—

"It is too late to burn her now. The Yankee is almost on board of us. We must surrender!" . . . Suddenly, with a deep humming sound, came a hundred-pound bolt. This shot was fired from their long gun amid-ships, and passed just over my head, between myself and the captain, who was standing on the bridge a little above me.

"By Jove! don't they intend to give us quarter, or show us some mercy at any rate?" cried Captain H. "I have surrendered."

And now from the Yankee came a stentorian hail: "Steamer ahoy! haul down that flag, or we will pour a broadside into you!"

Captain H. then ordered the man at the wheel to lower the colors; but he replied, with true British pluck, that "he had sailed many times under that flag, but had never yet seen it hauled down; and," added he, "I cannot do it now." We were sailing under British colors, and the man at the helm was an Englishman. . . . At last, some one, I know not who, seeing how hopeless it must be . . . lowered the English ensign.

Before the acknowledgment of our surrender had been made, a keg containing some twenty or thirty thousand dollars, equivalent in value to about six thousand pounds sterling, had been brought up on deck and consigned to the deep; whilst all my dispatches and letters of introduction, of which latter I had many, were consumed in the furnaces very shortly afterwards.

We were boarded by a boat's crew from our captor, under the command of the executive officer, Mr. Kempf. Mounting the side, he walked up to Captain H. and said—

"Good day to you, Captain; I am glad to see you. This is a very fine vessel, and a valuable one. Will you be good enough to let me see your papers?"

To this Captain H. replied, "Good day to yourself, sir; but as to my being happy to see you, I cannot really say that I am. I have no papers."

The Federal Lieutenant then said, "Well, Captain, your presence is required on board the United States steamer *Connecticut*." . . . Without further parley the two stepped together into the boat which was lying alongside, and immediately pulled for the *Connecticut*.

One Mr. Swasey was left in charge of our luckless *Greyhound*—an officer as unfit for authority as any who has ever trodden the deck of a man-of-war. His subordinates were, I imagine, well acquainted with his character and abilities; at all events, they treated his orders not with respect, but ridicule.

"Now, sergeant," said he, addressing the sergeant of marines, "look out for your men, and I will look out for mine. By-the-way, though, station one man here to guard the spirit-room, and don't let any one go below; the first man I catch doing so I will blow his brains out, I will; I would not let my own father have a drink."

He might possibly have resisted the solicitations of a thirsty parent, but he proved quite unable to withstand those of the men. He had hardly finished speaking, when a seaman, whom, by his *illigant* brogue, I recognized at once for a true son of Erin, approached and addressed Mr. Swasey with all the native eloquence and pathos of his country—

"Ah, Mr. Swasey, will yees be afther lettin' me have a small bottle of whiskey to kape out the could?"

The colloquy that ensued was ludicrous in the extreme, terminating in a victory of the Irish sailor over the Federal officer. This example of successful insubordination once set, was soon followed; and in every instance Mr. Swasey yielded to the remonstrances, or rather to the mutinous appeals, of his men.

"Here," suddenly exclaimed he, catching a glimpse of myself, "sergeant of the guard! sergeant of the guard! put a man in front of this door, and give him orders to stab this woman if she dares to attempt to come out."

This order, so highly becoming an officer and a gentleman, so courteous in its language, and withal so necessary to the safety and preservation of the prize, was given in a menacing voice and in the very words I have used. I record them for the purpose of showing how admirably the Federal Government has selected its naval officers, and how punctually and gallantly they fulfilled the instructions of their superiors. . . .

Mr. Swasey then came to the cabin-door and introduced himself in these brief but delicate words—"Now, ain't ye skeared?"

My blood was roused, and I replied, "No, I am not; I was never frightened at a Yankee in my life!"

This retort of mine seemed to surprise him, as he walked away without another word. The effects of his displeasure, however, soon made themselves felt. To my ineffable disgust, the officers, and even the men, were permitted to walk at pleasure into my cabin, which I had hoped would have been respected as the sanctuary of a modest girl. In this hope, as in so many others, I calculated far too much upon the forbearance and humanity of Yankees; and these qualities were seldom exhibited when their enemies were defenceless, and, consequently, at their mercy.

While these scenes were being enacted, my maid, and a colored woman whom Captain H. was conveying to a lady in Bermuda, were subjected to the rude familiarities of the prize crew.

At this moment one of the *Connecticut*'s officers, a Mr. Reveille, walked up to me and said, "Do you know that it was I who fired the shot that passed close over your head?"

"Was it?" replied I. "Should you like to know what I said of the gunner?"

"I should like to know."

"That man, whoever he may be, is an arrant coward to fire on a defenceless ship after her surrender."

To this rejoinder of mine, more sincere, perhaps, than prudent, he made no reply, but left the cabin with an embarrassed laugh.[10]

The official record shows that the Anglo-rebel steamer *Greyhound* was boarded at 1:40 P.M. on May 10th, having run the blockade the night before from Wilmington on route to Bermuda loaded with cotton, tobacco, and turpentine. Among her passengers was the famous rebel lady, Miss Belle Boyd, and her servant, and that between 6:00 and 8:00 P.M. a prize crew was placed aboard in charge of Acting Ensign Samuel Hardinge.[11]

Commander Almy's report noted, "The Captain represents himself as George Henry, but his real name is George H. Bier, whom I formerly knew as a Lieutenant in the U. S. Navy, and his name appears in the Confederate Navy register as a lieutenant in that service."[12]

Romance

10-15 MAY 1864

I beg you will consider yourself
a passenger, not a prisoner!
—S. Hardinge

BELLE NOTICED A YOUNG Union officer who boarded the *Greyhound*. He crossed the deck by the wheel, and approached the cabin.

> I saw at a glance he was made of other stuff than his com-
> rades . . . my attention was riveted by the presence of a
> gentleman—the first . . . whom I had met in the hour of my
> distress. . . . His dark brown hair hung down on his
> shoulders; his eyes were large and bright. Those who judge
> of beauty by regularity of feature only, could not have pro-
> nounced him strictly handsome. . . . [He was not] a model of
> Grecian grace; but the fascination of his manner was such,
> his every movement was so much that of a fine gentleman,
> that my "Southern proclivities," strong as they were, yielded
> for a moment to the impulses of my heart, and I said to
> myself, "Oh, what a good fellow that must be!"

He passed Belle's cabin, and to her secret disappointment, neither entered nor made inquiries about her. She asked another officer the name of the new arrival. "He is Lieutenant Hardinge" [pronounced Harding]. Soon afterwards, Belle overheard the following conversation with Mr. Swasey.

"Hallo, Hardinge, anything up? What is it?"

"Yes sir, by order of Captain Almy, I have come to relieve you of the command of this vessel," Hardinge responded. "It is his order that you proceed on board the *Connecticut*: you will be pleased to hand over to me the papers you have in relation to this vessel."

"It is a lie! It is a lie! It ain't no such thing! I won't believe it. You have been lately juggling with the captain. Confound it! That is the way you always do."

"Mr. Swasey, I am but obeying my orders; you must not insult me. If you continue to do so, I shall report you."

Swasey cooled at once, handing over his orders, jumping into the waiting boat, and returning to the *Connecticut*. Before long, Hardinge came aft, bowed, and asked permission to enter Belle's cabin.

"Certainly. I know that I am a prisoner," Belle replied.

"I am now in command of this vessel, and I beg you will consider yourself a passenger, not a prisoner."

From the time that Hardinge assumed command, the conduct of the crew underwent a complete change. A Union officer remarked that, although Hardinge was young, he knew how to command other men; he had learned early in life the secret and the value of discipline.

The officers and crew of the *Greyhound* were taken on board the *Connecticut*. Captain Henry, the steward, cook, the cabin boy, and Belle and her maid remained on the *Greyhound*. At eight o'clock that night the *Greyhound* was ordered to proceed north, keeping just astern of the *Connecticut*.

Before we were taken—indeed, when we sailed from Wilmington—it had been agreed that "Belle Boyd" should be for the time ignored, and that "Mrs. Lewis" should take her place. It was obvious that, in the event of capture, I should run less risk, suffer fewer privations, and be exposed to less indignity, under an assumed name. Conceive, then, my surprise and indignation when I found that my secret had been revealed through the treachery of an unworthy countryman!

Captain H. told me that the *Minnie*, a blockade-runner like the *Greyhound*, which had been captured the day before by the *Connecticut*, had been the means of our own mishap. There can be no doubt that one of her officers was a traitor to the cause of his country, and had, through fear, or actuated by some other unworthy motive, sacrificed those he should have defended with his life.

It is with reluctance that I record this instance of dishonor on the part of a Southerner; but I am resolved to be an impartial historian, and although often severe to the Yankees, by dint of telling plainly their short-comings, I will not shrink from the truth when it is unfavorable to my countrymen.

Belle retired to her cabin, tired and heartsick at the turn the tide of fortune had taken. Images of prison tormented her through the night; before dawn she finally succumbed to a light sleep.

The next morning, at daylight, I was aroused by loud hailing from the Yankee cruiser as she passed close to us, ordering that we should "heave-to" whilst she sent a boat on board. We presently learned that our destination was to be Fortress Monroe. . . .

It was the second evening after our surrender that Captain H., Mr. Hardinge, and myself, were seated together close by the wheel. The moon shone beautifully clear, lighting up every thing with a brightness truly magnificent; the ocean, just agitated by a slight breeze that swept over its surface, looked like one vast bed of sparkling diamonds, and the rippling of the little waves, as they struck the vessel's side, seemed but a soft accompaniment to the vocal music with which Captain H. had been regaling us.

Presently Captain H. went forward on the bridge. . . . We two were left to ourselves; and Mr. Hardinge quoted some beautiful passages from Byron and Shakespeare. Then, in a decidedly Claude Melnotte style, he endeavored to paint the "home to which, if love could but fulfil its prayers, this heart would lead thee!" And from poetry he passed on to plead an oft-told tale. . . .

Situated as I was, and having known him for so short a time, a very practical thought flitted through my brain. If he felt all that he professed to feel for me, he might in future be useful to us; so when he asked me "to be his wife," I told him that "his question involved serious consequences," and that "he must not expect an answer until I should arrive at Boston."

This seemingly lukewarm reception of his avowal did not dampen Hardinge's ardor in the least. Throughout the remainder of the voyage, he was as kind and courteous as though Belle had accepted him. Even Captain Henry took a great fancy to him and swore eternal friendship to "the most thorough gentleman from Yankeeland that he had ever met."

I sat on the little deck aft, watching with interest all that I saw, and listening alternately to the captain and Mr. Hardinge as they conversed on various topics. From the latter I ascertained that General Butler was in command at Fortress Monroe, and from him I could expect but little courtesy.

As we neared our anchorage, I made out distinctly the grim outline of the fortress, rising in its majesty and strength. I compared myself to the fly nearing the cunning old spider, who was eagerly watching for the moment when it should become entangled in his intricate web.

But such was not to be. They anchored close by the ironclad *Roanoke*, and a quite inebriated Commodore Guerte Gansevoorte swaggered aboard.

When the Commodore approached my cabin door, I heard Mr. Hardinge say, "Sir, a lady is dressing there. Will you be kind enough to wait? She is my passenger, and I am responsible for her." I had finished, however; and the colored servant, opening the door, said to Mr. Hardinge, "De lady am ready, massa." On this the Commodore remarked, "Ugh! got to that, has it?"

"So," said the Commodore, "this is Miss Belle Boyd, is it?"

The Commodore at first would not be seated, but did so after a few moments' further conversation. Champagne and glasses were brought in; and he soon became exceedingly communicative, and, with an oath, swore that Captain H. should have a parole extending as far as Boston. Asking for pen, ink, and paper, which I immediately procured, he bade the executive officer write the required parole, and signed it with his own hand. Mr. Hardinge asked for the document, or, at least, a copy of the same; but he would not comply, declaring that "his orders were sufficient."

As he rose to depart, he turned to me and said, in answer to a request of mine, "You, Miss, when you arrive at New York, can go on shore, provided Mr. Hardinge accompanies you. And," he added, attempting some compliments, "I will not enforce a written parole with you, but will take a verbal promise. Don't be at all alarmed—you shan't go to prison." The Commodore then left us. . . .

Half an hour may have passed, when a boat came from the *Roanoke* to inform Mr. Hardinge that the Commodore had ordered that the *Greyhound* should be brought under the lee of the iron-clad. My heart sank, for it seemed that, after all, he had been playing with us; still more so when, as we rounded-to under the *Roanoke*'s stern, I head the Commodore threatening through his trumpet to blow us out of the water. In his [drunken] condition he might have done any thing; so our anxiety may well be imagined.

As we lay beside the *Roanoke*, vague threats were made, and contradictory orders given. Now we were told to be "off at once," then "not to think of moving at present;" until Mr. Hardinge grew restless at such constant supervision, and, taking advantage of a command to quit the station, steamed away, without waiting for any thing more. Right glad were we when the shades of night hid from our view the monster ironclad. . . .

New York and Boston

15-31 MAY 1864

*What a contrast did . . . New York afford
. . . to my own sorrow-stricken land.*[1]

FINALLY THE *GREYHOUND* proceeded to sea, bound for Boston with an intermediate stop at New York for coaling. As the steamer approached New York, Belle had a commanding view of the harbor while seated beside Hardinge in the deck house. The panorama of sea and shore was breathtaking, unequalled, she felt, in beauty by the approach to any other city in the world.

The *Greyhound* proceeded up the East River and anchored off the Navy yard. Lieutenant Hardinge went ashore to report their arrival while the steamer took on coal.

> When Mr. Hardinge returned in the afternoon, the dock was filled with gazers, who, excited by that morbid curiosity exhibited by the world in general, had come to witness, as they supposed, my debarkation. In this they were somewhat disap-pointed, for every thing had been arranged so nicely that not one of the many there assembled knew when I went on shore. . . .
>
> Captain H. and Mr. Hardinge accompanied me. We crossed to the New York side of the river, and landed at the foot of Canal Street. Procuring a carriage, we drove to a friend's house, where I took from off my person the money

which I had concealed about me, and the weight of which at times had almost made me faint. This money belonged to myself and Captain H., and was not, as Yankee papers averred, part of the ship's money we had thrown overboard previous to our capture. Captain H. placed our money in the bank, where it was safe from further molestation.

We visited Niblo's Theatre, to witness the performance of "Bel Demonio." What a contrast did the gay, wealthy city of New York afford at this period to my own sorrow-stricken land! Here there was no sign of want or poverty. No woebegone faces could I see in that assemblage: all was life and animation. Though war raged within a short distance, its horrors had little influence on the butterflies of the Empire City; whilst, in my own dear native country, all was sad and heart-rending. We were sacrificing lives upon the altar of Liberty; while the North sacrificed hers upon the altar of Mammon.

The next morning Hardinge called for Belle, and they went shopping in the famous stores of New York City. All too soon they returned to the *Greyhound*, and about 4:00 P.M. the steamer sailed for Boston.

The weather was lovely, the water smooth as glass, and the sky cloudless as that of Italy. On each side of us, along the shores of the Sound, were beautiful residences, whose owners, as they strolled over their lawns, or sat smoking on terrace or balcony, appeared to think little, and care less, about the war. We glided past many craft, which lay with white sails that flapped against their masts. I was melancholy; I hardly knew why. The face of Nature wore its very sweetest smile; every thing was propitious; yet I was not pleased, and sought the cabin.

Mr. Hardinge, in a few moments, followed me, and then he repeated a declaration on which I need not expatiate, as it concerned ourselves more than any one else. So generous and noble was he in every thing, that I could not but acknowledge that my heart was his. I firmly believe that God intended us to meet and love; and, to make the story short, I told him that "I would be his wife." Although our politics differed, "Women," thought I, "can sometimes work wonders; and may not he, who is of Northern birth, come by degrees to love, for my sake, the ill-used South?"

Then Captain "Henry" came into the cabin; and, when we told him all, he joined our hands together, saying—

"Hardinge, you are a good fellow, and I love you, boy! Miss Belle deserves a good husband; and I know no one more worthy of her than yourself. May you both be happy!"

Despite Belle's romance, she never gave up the idea of escape. Shortly after the *Greyhound* was captured, Belle and the others agreed that an attempt should be made to regain control of the vessel, but the project had been abandoned, not from lack of zeal, but from force of circumstances. The aid of the chief engineer of the blockade runner was necessary to the operation of the ship, but his return to the *Greyhound* had been refused.

Another plan had better luck. Shortly before they arrived in Boston, Captain Henry discussed with Belle his plan for escape. He had friends there who would help, but he needed Belle's diversion of Hardinge's attention. It would not, he assured her, injure Hardinge, as the latter's responsibility ended at Boston, and so did Captain Henry's parole. It was now or never.

> . . . Mr. Hardinge was forward, giving orders to the men; Captain "Henry," Mr. Pollard, and myself were aft, seated in the cabin. I asked the two Yankee pilots if they would join us and partake of a glass of wine. To this they of course assented, and drank freely; for doubtless such wine but seldom passed their lips. I then nodded to Captain "Henry," who, carelessly putting on his hat, and taking his umbrella in his hand, walked up on deck and went aft, where he stood for some moments. Every thing seemed to favor us, for Mr. Hardinge had called a harbor-boat alongside, that he might go ashore to report his arrival.
>
> Before starting, Mr. Hardinge came to me and asked "where his papers were;" when I replied that I thought they must be "in the lower cabin, where he had been dressing himself." He immediately went down to fetch them; and this was the golden opportunity for which we had waited. In less time than it takes me to write it, Captain "Henry" stepped into the boat, which dropped slowly astern with the tide; and

when Mr. Hardinge reappeared, the Captain was safe on land.

The whole scene was amusing in the extreme to those who understood it, so well had it been managed. When Mr. Hardinge found his boat gone, he came to the conclusion that the waterman had grown tired of waiting and had pulled off; so, calling another, he stepped into it and proceeded to report his prize.

In about three hours he returned, bringing with him the United States Marshal, Keyes, and several other gentlemen of position and influence in Boston, whom he introduced to me.

The Marshal then asked for Captain Henry.

"I think he is on deck," I replied.

Mr. Hardinge went to find him, leaving the other gentlemen to converse with Mr. Pollard and myself. From me, however, they did not learn much, for I sustained the supposititious character of "Mrs. Lewis" with becoming gravity; and it was not until several days after that they became quite sure that I was none other than the celebrated "Belle Boyd."

In a few moments Marshal Keyes, followed by Mr. Hardinge, entered the cabin, the Marshal exclaiming, "Captain 'Henry' has escaped!"

"What!" said I; "it is impossible! Only a few moments ago he was here!" and I looked very serious, though all the while I was laughing in my sleeve, saying to myself, "Again I have got the better of the Yankees!" The vessel was thoroughly searched—nay, I believe that it was fumigated, or "smoked," to get the Captain out; for Marshal Keyes was "positive" that he was on board—so he informed me on his way to the hotel.

Captain "Henry's" escape caused much sensation. Detectives, great and small, were thrown into a flutter of excitement, and the Boston police, whom Marshal Keyes affirmed to be the "best in the world," were all astir, that the fugitive might be lodged in Fort Warren. These myrmidons of Northern power were, certainly, not favored with a very accurate description of Captain "Henry." Some declared that he wore a black hat, others that he had a white covering to his head; some that his nose was aquiline, others that it was decidedly *retroussé* [turned-up]. Such contradictions bewildered the police, whose efforts resulted in a wild-goose chase.

Late on the evening of the escape, Marshal Keyes was jubilant over a supposed capture at Portland, Maine, whither he had telegraphed to have any suspicious character arrested. The Portland captive proved to be not the gentleman of whom they were in quest, but a harmless English tourist, who was, no doubt, much aggrieved at his unlawful detention.

When the Marshal informed me of the Captain's arrest at Portland, I knew that there must be some mistake, and could hardly restrain my laughter; for all this time Captain "Henry" was lying *perdu* [concealed] in Boston, under an assumed name. I was well aware of the Captain's residence, and through the medium of a friend received several communications from him. In my replies I assured him that he was already as good as free. For two days he stayed quietly at the hotel, and then I heard that he had set off for Canada, *viâ* New York. Detectives had been sent all over the country to intercept him, but it was one of the best-managed escapes from the toils of the "cute" Yankees that ever took place. Captain "Henry" actually remained for some time at one of the largest hotels in Broadway, where he saw many of his old friends, who, fortunately, did not recognize him.

The *Greyhound* was hauled alongside a wharf, and an immense concourse of people assembled to witness my coming ashore; for it had been telegraphed from New York, and then again from the station in Boston Bay, that "Belle Boyd" was aboard the prize. Marshal Keyes was most courteous, and stated that he had procured a suite of rooms for me at the Tremont House, where I was to remain until my fate was definitely settled. This, he added, would be in a very few days; when he should either have the "supreme pleasure" of taking me to Canada, or the "unpleasant task" of delivering me over to the tender mercies of the commandant of Fort Warren.

The public journals were indefatigable in noticing all my movements. The Sunday-morning papers informed their readers that "Miss Belle Boyd would attend Divine service at the Old ___ Church during the forenoon." The week-day news-sheets gave notice that "Miss Belle Boyd, in company with her gallant captor, whose sympathies, no doubt, were with the South, were seen out driving the day before;" and, as a climax, the bulletin-boards announced that "Belle Boyd had been sent to the Fitchburg Jail!" Such were a few of the many *canards* [fabricated stories] that flew abroad during my stay in the "modern Athens."

I had been there about ten days, when Mr. Hardinge, fearing that the "Fitchburg Jail" story might be but the shadow of a coming event, proceeded to Washington, to procure, if possible, my release. Having letters of introduction to many of the leading and influential men there, he induced them to use their power in my behalf.

Although I was but thirty-six hours' railway-journey from my mother, who had telegraphed to the Marshal to allow her to come and see me, she was not permitted to do so; and none of her letters reached me, they being probably intercepted. But, if letters of affection were thus stopped, there were, happily, other channels than the postal department by which friendly comfort could arrive. Many Boston ladies and gentlemen visited me, despite the Government spies who hovered about my quarters.

After being kept in suspense for three weeks, I forwarded, through Marshal Keyes, a letter to Gideon Welles, Secretary of the Navy at Washington, telling him that "I really was Belle Boyd, and wished to go to Canada, that I might communicate with my mother."

The Marshal received a telegram in answer, saying that "Miss Boyd and her servants should be escorted beyond the lines into Canada," and that, *if I was again caught in the United States, or by the United States authorities, I should be shot*. This was on a Sunday evening; and the Marshal advised me to depart with all convenient speed, as I had only twenty-four hours' grace. I promised to start on Monday, at five P.M. It was impossible to go sooner, no trains running through to Montreal on Sunday.

The *Washington Republican* got possession of my letter to Gideon Welles, and published it *in extenso* [in its entirety], with the remark that I was "insane," and had been, on that account, released by the Government. For this verdict of lunacy I thank them, if it contributed in any degree to mitigate my sentence. There certainly existed sufficient method in my madness to make me appreciate the advantage of having the promised shooting deferred until they caught me again; and I felt much obliged to members of Congress and others who used their influence in my behalf.

Mr. Hardinge was sent for early on Monday morning by Admiral [Silas H.] Stringham, but he assured me that he would soon return. The day passed by, however, without any sign of him, and I began to wonder what had happened, when I received the following letter in his handwriting:

"My dear Miss Belle,

"It is all up with me. Mr. Hall, the engineers, and myself, are prisoners, charged with complicity in the escape of Captain H____. The Admiral says that it looks bad for us; so I have adopted a very good motto, viz: 'Face the music!' and, come what may, the officers under me shall be cleared. I have asked permission of the Admiral to come and bid you good-by. I hope that this answer will be in the affirmative."

This was written on board the receiving-ship *Ohio*. Its receipt made me feel very unhappy, for I feared that circumstantial evidence was against Mr. Hardinge, and that, ere long, he would, although perfectly innocent, share with poor Mr. Pollard[2] a casemate in Fort Warren. But suddenly the object of my thoughts made his appearance. He informed me that the Admiral had allowed him and his officers to be paroled until sundown, and that he had availed himself of this privilege to come instantly to me. . . .

The time for my departure from Boston came at last. The Tremont Hotel was left, and the railway dépôt was reached. Marshal Keyes endeavored to make himself agreeable, and was very busy in getting my baggage checked and my ticket taken before the train moved away. The Marshal, I may add, was my courteous companion to the boundary-line between Canada and the United States. With a sad heart I had bidden good-by to Mr. Hardinge, although I trusted that he would soon rejoin me; and I enjoyed the delightful prospect of breathing free Canadian air.

Yes, I should be free! Free from prison bars and irksome confinement; but alas! an exile! Each step towards freedom carried me farther and farther from my native land; whilst, did I turn back, a heavy penalty awaited me. My father dead, and my dear mother far away! Truly I was alone in the wide, wide world! And I had left one generous heart behind that I knew would miss me sorely.

PART SEVEN

Freedom

(1864)

Brunswick Hotel. Jermyn St. London
24th Jany 1865—

Hon'ble. Abraham Lincoln
President of the U.S. America

I have heard from good authority that if
I suppress the Book I have now ready for
publication, you may be induced to consider
favorably the case of my husband, I ought to
say Harding, now a prisoner in Fort Delaware.
I think it would be well for you & me to
come to some definite understanding—
My Book was not originally intended to
be more than a personal narrative, but since
my husband's unjust arrest I had intended
making it political, & had introduced many

obvious circumstances respecting your
Government with which I am so well
acquainted which would open the
eyes of Europe to many things to which
the world on this side of the water little
dreams— If you will release my
husband & set him free, so that he may
join me here in England by the beginning
of March— I pledge you my word that my
Book shall be suppressed. Should my
Book be suppressed & husband not be with me by the 25th of
March I shall at once place my Book in
the hands of a publisher.
Trusting an immediate reply,

I am Sir, Yr. obdt. Servt
Belle Boyd Harding

Belle Boyd's Letter to Abraham Lincoln. (Courtesy of Library of Congress; reproduced from the February 1948 issue of the Lincoln Herald.)

CHAPTER TWENTY-FIVE

The Exile

JUNE—AUGUST 1864

*Spies were stationed on the bridge
. . . to entrap us, should we by chance be foolish enough. . . .*[1]

IN MONTREAL I MET many Southern families, refugees, and many Confederate sympathizers. The British provinces were at this time a haven of rest for American exiles—much as England has always been to the victims of persecution on the European continent. I learned that my friends at Niagara [Captain Henry and spouse] were expecting me, and accordingly set off to join them, the Guards serenading me just before my departure.

Niagara, with its sublime scenery, I will not attempt to describe. We were stopping at the Clifton House, and from my windows I could plainly see the Yankee side of the Falls. There, lower down, was the Suspension Bridge, offering almost irresistible temptation to cross from Canada to the States. We heard, on good authority, that above a hundred thousand dollars was being expended on the retaking of Captain "Henry" and myself. Spies were stationed on the bridge to watch, and, if possible, to entrap us, should we by chance be foolish enough to venture within their power.

About a week after our arrival at Niagara we noticed, at the *table d'hôte*, two very foppishly-dressed men, with thin, waxed mustaches *à la Napoléon*, and who apparently took great seeming interest in the movements of our entire party. We watched them closely, and were very soon convinced beyond doubt that they were Yankee detectives. Shortly after this discovery, we left for Quebec. It was in the morning, about eight o'clock, that we quitted Niagara and proceeded by rail to Toronto, where we arrived about noon. Imagine our surprise at finding the fair imitation dandies, whom we had left quietly at the "Clifton House," watching for us at the Toronto terminus! It transpired that they had seen us going, and had quietly entered another car in the same train.

The Canadian journals commented severely upon these fellows, and the system of espionage practised on us whilst we remained in the provinces.

The brace of detectives accompanied us in the steamer that left Toronto a few hours afterwards, and which plies regularly during the summer months between that place and Montreal. We noticed that they hovered round, eyeing us narrowly; and we determined to ascertain whether it was really our party that they were watching. When, therefore, we arrived at our destination, Captain "Henry" repaired to the "Donegana Hotel," whilst I went to the "St. Lawrence Hall." In a few hours I learned that one of these fellows had engaged a room at the same hotel where I was stopping; and, when Captain "Henry" called, he told me that the other detective had taken up his abode at the "Donegana"!

The Union agents followed Belle everywhere. Captain Henry suggested that she go to Europe for sanctuary, leaving from Quebec. The idea seemed fine to Belle, so Captain Henry sought out some Confederate agents who obtained funds for her trip. The Henrys accompanied her to Quebec.

Upon their arrival, the detectives were still with them. Captain Henry and his wife left for Halifax, but Belle remained in Quebec, awaiting a vessel to Europe. When she finally left for England, one of the detectives actually tried to secure passage on that vessel, but Canadian authorities refused.

My trip across the Atlantic was, on the whole, favored by calm weather and a smooth sea; so that I did not suffer much from my enemy, the *mal de mer*. Off the banks of Newfoundland we were, to make use of a nautical expression, "tied up" for more than a week by the fogs, amid fields and bergs of ice. The latter I had never before seen; and I gazed upon their majestic grandeur with feelings of awe and amazement. So near, at times, did we pass them, that it is no wonder that I felt somewhat nervous; for, had we struck, it would have been instantaneous death to us all. While crossing the banks we encountered a fearful storm, and for one entire night the steamer rolled and plunged with the force of the waves like some living creature.

When, after entering English waters and passing up the Channel, and my feet touched the ground once more, I thanked God for our safety. . . .

Arrived in Liverpool, I remained there for some days at the Washington Hotel, and then proceeded to London. I soon ascertained the address of Mr. Hotze, the Confederate commercial agent, to whom I had letters of introduction from the Secretary of State. I reported to the Confederate States Commissioner that the dispatches intrusted to me at Wilmington had been destroyed when the *Greyhound* was overhauled, that they might not fall into our enemy's hands.

From the time that Belle left Boston, she had been in a constant state of anxiety regarding Sam Hardinge, blaming herself for his capture. Though she did not yet know it, Hardinge had been released and was himself in Europe! According to the records of the Navy Department, Hardinge was arrested by order of the Secretary of the Navy on 8 June, was confined on board the *Ohio* until 8 July, and on that same day was dismissed from the service:

> For your neglect of duty, in permitting the Captain of the prize steamer *Greyhound* under your charge to escape, you are hereby dismissed from the Navy of the United States as an Acting Ensign on temporary service.[2]

His dismissal may have been more complex than the records show. He may have, in fact, resigned. Or his release may have been the fruit of extortion: Belle had a wide knowledge of undercover activities of politicians in Washington, and hinted that she had such knowledge and could be driven to use it. In his introduction to *Belle Boyd in Camp and Prison*, George Sala threatened:

> [Belle Boyd] is in possession of a vast amount of information implicating high officials at Washington both in public and private scandals, which she deems it imprudent at present to publish. The time is not yet![3]

Hardinge's release may have resulted from a tacit understanding that, if Belle got him back, she would keep silent.

> Mr. Hotze gave me a letter that had been left with him until I should reach London. Upon opening it, I found that it was from Mr. Hardinge, informing me that he had come to England, but not being able to learn my whereabouts, had proceeded to Paris, in the faint hope of finding me there. I was deeply touched at this new proof of his honest attachment, and immediately telegraphed a message to him, stating where he would find me in London. Gentle reader, you, perhaps, imagine for yourself how joyful was our meeting, and in what manner a courtship, which had in it much of romance, was, at length, happily terminated.[4]

To Have and to Hold . . .

25 AUGUST—22 SEPTEMBER 1864

Hail, wedded love, mysterious law,
true source of human offspring.
—John Milton[1]

BELLE SPENT THE NEXT few days preparing for the wedding. There were visits to her dressmaker, a call at the rectory of St. James Chapel in Piccadilly, arrangements for flowers and the wedding cake, and endless details. In addition to this business, there were parties, luncheons, teas, and dinners. The "Southern colony" in London included merchants, shippers, journalists, military officers, and diplomatic agents. Belle had met and worked with most of them, and as a popular member of the colony, included them on the invitation list.[2]

Mr. Henry Hotze, the Confederacy's commercial agent in Britain, took Belle under his wing, introducing her to the many American representatives in London who, when the war began, stayed abroad to work for the Confederacy. They were responsible for the English-built ships destined for the South. Belle joined this horde of workers and was included in their social functions.

News of the approaching ceremony found its way into the British newspapers, which alarmed Belle, as she feared that the attention might somehow hurt the Southern cause. (This fear is revealed in a letter to President Davis, reproduced later in this chapter.) The length and the tone of some of the reports made her uneasy, but Hotze made light of her fears, saying that the articles would have a positive influence on her work in England. Belle quotes a newspaper article:

(*Morning Post.*) "St. James's Church, Piccadilly, was yesterday the scene of a romantic episode in the fratricidal war now raging on the American continent; as, at the altar of that sacred edifice, Miss Belle Boyd, whose name and fame are deservedly cherished in the Southern States, pledged her troth to Mr. Sam Wylde Hardinge, formerly an officer in the Federal naval service. The marriage attracted to the church a considerable number of English and American sympathizers in the cause of the South, anxious to see the lady whose heroism has made her name so famous, and to witness the result of her last captivity, the making captive of the Federal officer under whose guard she was again being conveyed to prison. Miss Boyd, it will be remembered, is the Virginian lady who, during the terrible scenes enacted in the Valley of the Shenandoah, rendered such essential service to General Stonewall Jackson, by procuring for him information of great value as regards the position and condition of the Northern forces, and who signalized her devotion to the cause of her country by so many other services. Capture and imprisonment did not damp her adventurous and patriotic ardor, as she was twice immured; once for seven months, and once for ten months. She was again seized, and, while on board a Federal vessel, on her way to the North, made the acquaintance of Lieutenant Hardinge, with whom, having crossed the Atlantic, she has entered into the bonds of matrimony. Mr. Hardinge needs no excuse for the step he has taken in renouncing his allegiance to the Federal cause and espousing the fair 'Rebel', whom he has now sworn to love, honor, and cherish. Though, in obedience to the wishes of his father, he served for some time in the Federal navy, in which service he rose to be lieutenant, his Southern sympathies were notorious in the North, where it was well known that he had long tendered his resignation, which Mr. Secretary Welles refused to accept; and thus he was forced to continue in a service which he would gladly have renounced long since. Though more than suspected of Southern sympathies, he kept his word when he promised the executive of the Federal navy that the name he bore—a name which had descended to him from a long line of ancestors in Great

Britain and America—should not be disgraced, and proved his readiness to perform his duty on many occasions.

"The bride was attended to the altar by Mrs. Edward Robinson Harvey, the bridegroom by Mr. Henry Howard Barber, and the marriage service was read by the Rev. Mr. Paull, of St. James's Chapel, in a manner which deeply impressed all present with the solemn nature of the contract entered into. Amongst the friends of the bride and bridegroom, and of the Confederate cause, who attended, were the Hon. General Williams, formerly United States Minister at Constantinople; the Hon. J. L. O'Sullivan, formerly Minister from Washington at Lisbon; Major Hughes, of the Confederate army; Captain Fearn, Confederate army; the Rev. Frederic Kill Harford (who gave the bride away); Mr. Keen Richards, of Kentucky; Mr. Henry Hotze, Mr. C. Warren Adams, Mrs. Paull, Madame Cerbelle, Mr. Reay, &c.

"At the conclusion of the ceremony, the bride and bridegroom, and their friends, proceeded to the Brunswick Hotel, Jermyn Street, where a choice and well-arranged breakfast was partaken of; and at a fitting moment, towards the conclusion, Mr. Barber, in a most eloquent speech, proposed the health of Mr. and Mrs. Hardinge, eulogizing the services the lady had performed, and prognosticating that the bridegroom would soon win fame in the service on which he is about to enter. The toast, as may be anticipated, was received with much delight, and was replied to by both bride and bridegroom, who expressed their acknowledgments to the many friends they had found in this country. The toast of 'The Queen' was afterwards given by Captain Fearn, who assured the English portion of his hearers that her Majesty was greatly revered in all parts of the Southern States of America—an assertion which was most warmly corroborated by all present, who were qualified to speak from experience. 'President Davis and General Lee,' and many other toasts, followed in due order, till the growing hours warned the bride and bridegroom that it was time to depart for Liverpool. Mr. Hardinge purposes in a few days to leave for the South, whither, in spite of the blockade, he intends to convey a goodly portion of the wedding cake, for distribution amongst his wife's friends."[3]

Our marriage took place on August 25th [1864], and journalists were pleased to treat the world to some portions of the romance in which we had taken part. The English press was friendly in its tone, but certain Yankee editors became marvellously indignant at the news, and even now they are subject to periodical returns of indignation.[4]

Legend is insistent that the Prince of Wales (later Edward VII) attended the wedding. Knowing his unconventional behavior, it is possible, but not probable, that he attended; no historical proof exists.[5] The presence of such personages as Henry Hotze, James Williams, and John L. O'Sullivan indicates that Belle ranked exceptionally high as an agent of the Confederacy.

"They were married and lived happily ever after" did not apply to Mr. and Mrs. Hardinge. After the wedding, Belle accompanied her husband to Liverpool and remained with him for about a week until his ship sailed for America.

Here Belle's book ends abruptly and is appended by *"Lieutenant Hardinge's Journal."* She decided to add it to her adventures as an "after-piece." There are five chapters, recounting his activities and reflections. His final paragraph reads,

> Many have advised me to suppress this volume, urging that its publication will probably cause my life-long banishment. But I cannot—I will not recede. I firmly believe that in this fiery ordeal, in this suffering, misery, and woe, the South is but undergoing a purification by fire and steel that will, in good time, and by His decree, work out its own aim.[6]

After the wedding and Hardinge's departure for America, Belle worried that her marriage to a Yankee might be resented in the Confederacy. She feared that it might diminish her influence, at home and abroad. So, she penned the following letter to President Davis:

Brunswick Hotel,
Jermyn Street, London.
Picadilly.
Sept. 22nd, 1864.

Hon. Jefferson Davis.

Dear Sir;

I suppose that the news of my marriage has been rec'd in the Confederacy. I send you a paper containing the English account of my wedding. My husband will soon be in the South where I trust he will meet a warm reception, and all *will forget* that he was once in the ranks of the enemy. I trust from my having married a man of Northern birth my Country will not doubt my loyalty. Though I loved him I asked the advice of Mr. Hotze and other Confederates here before I took the step, fearing that my Country would judge me wrong. Mr. Hardinge has given up all property and everything. His father is a Republican and has disinherited him for joining the *Southern Cause* and marrying a *Rebel.*

Do you think there will soon be peace? England wishes for it, and all here sympathize with the South. I have been met so kindly. Of yourself, and Stonewall Jackson and Gen'l Lee, the English have the greatest admiration and respect. If at any time I can be of benefit to my Country, command me.

Respectfully,
Your o'b't serv't,
Belle Boyd Hardinge,
CSA.[7]

PART EIGHT

Tragedy and a New Beginning

(1864-1900)

Belle Boyd's grave, Spring Grove Cemetery, Wisconsin Dells WI, on Memorial Day, 1953. Her stone is at lower right, beside picket fence. (Photo by H. H. Bennett Studio, Wisconsin Dells; used with permission.)

CHAPTER TWENTY-SEVEN

... Until Death Do Us Part

26 AUGUST 1864—APRIL 1865

I lay for a time thinking, looking into the fire . . .
and thinking of you sadly, far away from me
in England—the exile, lonely, and sad.
—Sam Hardinge's Journal[1]

HARDINGE RETURNED BY WAY of Boston and New York, visiting his parents in Brooklyn. He then left for Martinsburg to see Belle's family. When he arrived, Mrs. Boyd was away, but he spent a long, warm evening with Grandmother Glenn and slept that night in Belle's room.

> When, at last, I retired to sleep, it was in your own room; and as I entered in at the door, I uncovered my head, and thought of you.
>
> This was your room; here you had been held a prisoner, and had suffered the torture of an agonizing doubt as to your fate. Here lay your books just as you had left them. Writings, quotations, everything to remind me of you were here; and I do not know how long a time I should have stood gazing about me in silence, had it not been for my revery being disturbed by the little negro servant, who broke the silence by saying, "No one's ever sleep in dis room since Missy Bel' been gone—missus says you're de only purson as should."
>
> So, when I retired to bed that night, and "Jim" had been dismissed from further attendance upon me, I lay for a time thinking, looking into the fire, that glimmered and glared about the room, picturing you here, there, and everywhere

about the chamber, and thinking of you sadly, far away from me in England—the exile, lonely, and sad.[2]

Hardinge left Martinsburg the next afternoon for Baltimore. At Monocacy Station he was arrested and confined all night as a deserter. The next day he was sent to Harpers Ferry, and later to Washington and a "horrible hole," Forrest Hall prison. The prison was located in the suburb of Georgetown, once being a place of public entertainment. Now the walls were defaced with "unseemly pictures, vulgar writings, and punctured plaster." In a space about seventy-five feet square, dirty, ragged, filthy prisoners were crowded together. They had been there many months and were of all conditions and colors.

The prisoners called it "The Last Ditch" because it was considered the worst of the Federal prisons. Later Hardinge was moved to the Old Capitol and then placed in Carroll Prison, where Belle had languished a year before. He thought of her and the wretched days and nights she spent there.[3]

Hardinge's journal, "originally intended solely for the perusal of my wife," gives many details of the crude prison life and reveals the difficulty he had in adjusting to it. Superintendent Wood was still in charge of the Old Capitol and Carroll prisons; shortly after Hardinge's arrival, Wood saw him:

Ho, ho, here we are! So you're the husband of the famous Belle Boyd, are you? Well, we haven't got her, but we've got her husband, that's next to it![4]

Wood confided to Hardinge that he had a notebook of reminiscences about the Old Capitol, which, if published, would equal any of Reynold's novels about the Tower of London.[5]

Hardinge's experiences in prison were unpleasant; they weakened and depressed him. He was able to derive comfort and satisfaction from the consideration given him by other prisoners when they learned that he was Belle's husband. Meanwhile, Hardinge's parents had learned of his arrest and imprisonment and came to Washington to see him. They called on Secretary of War Stanton and obtained a pass. During their visit Hardinge discovered that he was to be sent to Fort Delaware, near Wilmington.[6]

The conditions of his imprisonment at Fort Delaware were even harsher than in Washington, and it is jarring to read of the cruelty and torture practiced by Americans against Americans. Hardinge was finally released on 3 February 1865, so weak he could hardly walk.

It was with feelings of unmistakable pleasure that I felt my feet pressing once more *terra firma*, and experienced the gratifying sensation awakening itself within me that I was once more my own master. So, drawing my tattered blanket about me, I stepped into the hotel that stood near the landing, and inquired the distance to Wilmington.

The proprietor of this country place eyed me suspiciously; the dog who had been basking at the fire rose and growled at me; and the frequenters of the place, who were seated round the stove smoking or drinking, by their looks inferred as plainly as tongue could speak, "He is an escaped prisoner." And no wonder, when I describe to you my presentation dress upon the occasion.

A felt hat, remarkable only for its being crownless, adorned my head; a ragged blanket sufficed—only in a measure, however—to keep the cold from my coatless body; a pair of "inexpressibles," horribly dilapidated, encased my lower extremities; a boot on one foot, and the other wrapped up in old rags. Is it a wonder, then, that I was an object of doubtful character?

Seating myself near the fire, I called for a glass of wine, which was handed to me by the bar-tender, who muttered something about a desire that he had of seeing "the color of my money."

To this I replied by drawing out my pocket-book, and offering him a fifty-dollar greenback, desiring him to give me small moneys for it. In an instant the conduct of those present underwent a complete change; the bar-tender was all smirks and bows, and, with an urbanity that was all the more strikingly apparent from his former behavior, desired to know if I wished to have an apartment.

"No, I wish to go to Wilmington. How far is it from here?"

"Sixteen miles," was the reply.

"Is there any conveyance that will take me there to-night?"

There was none.

"Hem! not if I will pay you well for it."

"I wouldn't let a dog of mine go out this night," was the answer.

"Then I will walk," I said.

"Walk!" was chorused simultaneously, with astonishment depicted on their countenances.

"Yes, walk!" I reiterated, desperately.

"Well, if you get to Wilmington safely, you will do more than I expect you will, in that garb especially;" and the speaker looked at my costume with a sneer.

"Nevertheless, I am going," I said; and, suiting the action to the word, I rose, and, attended to the door of the hotel by the group of astonished villagers, I commenced the journey.

It had been snowing and raining alternately throughout the day, and the roads in this part of the country, never at any time when I saw them remarkable for their goodness, were ankle-deep with mud. I shall never have the recollection of that night obliterated from my memory. Several times I was on the point of lying down on the roadside; but the love of life and the thought that—God willing—I should soon be at home, were strong within me, and I staggered on through the freezing rain and slushy snow.

Twice on the way I inquired at the door of some farmhouses the direction that I was to take, and once the "gude wife" of the quiet homestead where I gained admittance prepared for me with her own white hands a cup of coffee, and pressed me to stay all night at her hospitable place—an invitation in which she was seconded by the rest of the family. Herself and husband were both English, and I shall not forget their kindness to me; and when I at last rose to depart, the husband, wife, and children bade me a kind adieu, the husband accompanying me down the road some distance.

At last, just as the clock was striking ten, I staggered into the dépôt at Wilmington, just in time to catch the train for New York. I had accomplished the distance in four hours, but it was fully a week before I was able to walk or sit even with any degree of comfort.

Early in the morning I arrived in New York, and drove immediately to my brother's place of business. He was perfectly amazed at seeing me, and laughed immoderately at the deplorable figure I cut.

Eventually, having procured a suit of clothes, and enjoyed the luxury of a bath and the inexpressible feeling of delight that one has in finding his body once more in contact with clean linen, I bade adieu to the United States [on February 8th], and started directly for the shores of hospitable and peaceful England.[7]

Sam Hardinge's story ends sadly and mysteriously. Margaret Leech, in *Reveille in Washington*, states simply that "he went back to the United States soon after the marriage, and died without rejoining Belle."[8] However, Belle's cousin from Knoxville, Sue Boyd Barton, says that he was drowned at sea when a White Star Steamer went down.[9] Belle does not even mention his death in her memoirs; perhaps it was too painful for her or she was ignorant of the circumstances. George Sala, in his preface to *Belle Boyd in Camp and Prison*, quoted a newspaper report that Hardinge sailed for England on 8 February.[10] The addition of his *Journal* to Belle's book indicates that there was some communication from him; at least she received his memoirs.

Curtis Carroll Davis, in introductory remarks to his annotated reprint of *Belle Boyd in Camp and Prison*, notes, "When Sam Hardinge, abruptly and mysteriously released from Fort Delaware, at last arrived in London in late February or early March, 1865, he found that his wife had, in his absence, been alert to defend his good name." Davis then quotes a letter Belle wrote to the *Washington Evening Star* in defense of her husband. He adds: "In any event, after contributing his fragmentary journal to Belle's book, and siring her first-born child, Sam Hardinge disappears from notice forever."[11]

CHAPTER TWENTY-EIGHT

Belle's Letter to Abraham Lincoln

24 JANUARY 1865

*I think it would be well for you
and me to come to some definite understanding.
—Belle to Lincoln*

O N JANUARY 24, 1865 Belle wrote an extraordinary letter to President Lincoln. It was not until 1947 that the letter was found in the then recently opened Robert Todd Lincoln Collection of the Abraham Lincoln Papers in the Library of Congress. Its full text was first disclosed, in the *Lincoln Herald* in February of 1948, in an article by Louis Sigaud entitled "When Belle Boyd Wrote Lincoln."[1] Although the letter did reach the White House and was preserved by the President's son, Robert Todd, no answer to the letter has been found. It is probable that Lincoln himself read it; he may have been influenced by it.

Belle's literary style was as compelling as her personality, addressing President Lincoln as bluntly as she would any other mortal. The very first sentence of the letter may suggest that the first offer was made by Federal authorities. Belle, learning that they might consider "leniency" for Hardinge if she would suppress her book, was ready to state her terms.

Brunswick Hotel.
Jermyn St. London
24th. Jany. 1865

Honble Abraham Lincoln
    President of the U.S. America

I have heard from good authority that if I suppress the Book I have now ready for publication, you may be induced to consider leniently the case of my husband, S. Wylde Hardinge, now a prisoner in Fort Delaware, I think it would be well for you & me to come to some definite understanding. My Book was not originally intended to be more than a personal narrative, but since my husband's unjust arrest I had intended making it political, & had introduced many atrocious circumstances respecting your government with which I am so well acquainted & which would open the eyes of Europe to many things of which the world on this side of the water little dreams. If you will release my husband & set him free, so that he may join me here in England by the beginning of March—I pledge you my word that my Book shall be suppressed. Should my husband not be with me by the 25th of March I shall at once place my Book in the hands of a publisher.
Trusting an immediate reply,

I am Sir, Yr. obdt. Sevt.
Belle Boyd Hardinge

Belle's letter may throw light on why Hardinge was released without explanation. Her letter is dated 24 January 1865 and Hardinge was released ten days later on 3 February. The brief interval suggests immediate action and transatlantic mail service at the time could have delivered the letter well within ten days.[2] We also know that Lincoln was compassionate and may have ordered Hardinge's release because he considered the prisoner arrested and confined without legal grounds, on suspicion only, simply because he was Belle's husband. It is nice to think, too, that Lincoln might have admired the ingenuity and firmness of a woman of only twenty-one who had endured so much and who had the pluck to challenge the chief executive of the enemy.

Hardinge gives some insight into the cause of his imprisonment. In his *Journal* he records a Christmas Eve conversation with Major Levi C. Turner, investigator of the Judge Advocate's Department:

> "Can you inform me when I am to be released?"
> "Oh, one of these days."
> "Are there any charges against me?"
> "None sir; that is, perhaps there may be."
> "Then why am I held prisoner here?"
> "Because it pleases the Government."
> "Ah, but do you call it justice?"
> "Be careful what you say, sir. You are held here because it pleases Mr. Stanton; besides, your wife won't destroy any more of our army than she has done, Mr. H., if you are held as a hostage; and Mr. Stanton has an affectionate regard for your future welfare."
> "I repeat my question. Is it justice?"
> "Justice or not, we keep you here to make a patriot of you."[3]

Hardinge tells the story of his release in his *Journal*:

> . . . I was . . . ushered into the august presence of the comman-dant, who stared hard at me, without, however, saying any thing. One of his aides, evidently a secretary, handed me, after a few moments had elapsed, the following document, which was to be my safe-conduct by sea and land:
>
> Special Orders
> No. 62.
>
> Headquarters,
Fort Delaware, Del.,
Feb. 3d, 1865.
>
> S. Wilde Hardinge (Political Prisoner) is hereby released from confinement at this Post, in compliance with the follow-ing telegram from the War Department, dated Feb. 3d, 1865:—
>
> Brig.-Genl. A. Schoepf,
Fort Delaware

The Secretary of War directs the release of S. Wilde Hardinge, a Prisoner of Fort Delaware. Acknowledge receipt, and inform me when Mr. Hardinge leaves the island.

(Sgd.) James A. Hardee,
Col. and Insp.-Genl.

(Seal) A. Schoepf,
Brig.-Genl. Comg.[4]

The General then remarked, "Mr. H___, you have now our permission to leave the island. Will you go tonight or tomorrow morning? Do you go to Baltimore or New York City? I presume you will leave for Europe by the *first steamer?*"

Hardinge answered that his destination was New York City, and that he would remain no longer than necessary.

In ordering Hardinge's release, did Secretary Stanton act personally or by orders from Lincoln? Stanton usually opposed releases, but Lincoln sometimes overrode him. Significantly, the letter from Belle was not found in the files of the War Department, but in the Lincoln papers which were sealed for eighty years. Hardinge's release by official telegram shows that it was not routine procedure—immediate action was required in a specific case, including personal notification of compliance.[5]

The fact that Belle does not mention the letter to Lincoln in her memoirs is characteristic. Despite her ego, she was reticent on many subjects and was especially cautious with the life of her husband at stake. Had Lincoln known Belle personally, he probably would have approved her loyalty to those she loved and to the principles in which she believed. Further, the end of the war was near and Lincoln had many national problems to confront.

What facts Belle had meant to reveal were omitted when her book was finally published. It is highly probable that Stanton knew that Belle was aware of many actions in Washington that would create scandal if they were disclosed. It is more than hinted at in George Sala's preface to her book, which stated that Belle Boyd "is in possession of a vast amount of information implicating certain high officials at Washington both in public and private scandals, which she deems imprudent at present to publish. The time is not yet."[6]

Belle, like the great majority of people, was horrified by the assassination of Lincoln shortly after the war ended:

> Personally I had no animosity against the honorable gentleman who has wielded the sceptre of Northern power for four long years. His has been a trying position. No man probably in the pages of History took his seat under more inauspicious circumstances. The press of the world warred furious warfare upon him. He was jeered and scoffed at; he was pronounced uncouth, vulgar, low, servile, and abject; disappointed politicians and opposition cliques vied with each other in calling him on every occasion the "rail-splitter"; and wise-acres of soothsaying proclivities speedily predicted that, with such a man as Abraham Lincoln at the head of the Government, the Union would most assuredly be split, with as much precision and as quickly as Mr. Lincoln had been known to split rails when a backwoodsman in the Western wilds. . . . Now all is changed. Can anyone believe that Mr. Johnson is the man who is to restore the Republic to what it was, save the nation from bankruptcy, and bring peace and goodwill to America? It might not have been impossible with Mr. Lincoln; for that gentleman held out the olive branch, concealing no deadly weapon beneath it, to General Lee and his little band of heroes. . . . And, in truth, our people have more to regret in the death of President Lincoln than have the people of the North. When our old chieftain, General Lee, heard of the assassination he covered his face and refused to listen to the details of the murder. . . . There are those who will blame the South for this deed . . . but I appeal to Europe to judge discriminately between North and South. Do not pronounce too hastily your judgment, nor cast upon a brave and chivalrous people the stigma of assassination.[7]

Widow, Mother, Author

AUGUST 1864—DECEMBER 1866

Take this . . . publish it or burn it. . . .
It is the story of my adventures,
misfortunes, and persecution.[1]

WHEN SAM HARDINGE left England, Belle returned from Liverpool to London. She had enough money to support herself for awhile, but this was rapidly depleted. She sold most of her jewelry and wedding presents.[2]

Belle had dedicated her life to the Confederacy, but now it was a lost cause.[3] Desolate, depressed, and alone, her immediate problem was to support herself and to prepare for the birth of her child. What could she do? She was not trained for any profession. What services could she perform? Her only experience had been as a spy and courier, and there was little demand for those! She was too proud to accept charity from others. The thought of writing about her experiences emerged—why not sell the story of her life?[4]

So Belle spent the next few months writing her memoirs, working daily with little interruption. She stopped for an hour each day, if weather permitted, for a walk in the park, then returned to her task. Invitations from friends took second place to her work. Sometimes she had doubts about the wisdom of writing her book, and they were more than the usual insecurities experienced by new authors. She feared implicating those who had helped her. There was also the danger of jeopardizing her husband: if she did not publish the book, there was the possibility that he might be released from prison. But if she told the truth, he might be imprisoned for life or even given the death penalty. What should she do?[5]

Belle showed her manuscript to the famous English journalist and writer, George Augustus Sala. He had reported the war in America for the *Daily Telegraph* of London.

"Will you take my life?" Belle asked.[6] Startled by her desperate plea, George Sala, the friend of Dickens and Thackeray, stared in amazement at the young woman before him. "She was young, certainly no more than twenty-one years of age, with a tall, supple figure, light hair, and bright gray-blue eyes. Features, too irregular to be merely pretty, suggested firmness, and even joyous recklessness. Graceful, self-assured, and exquisitely gowned according to the latest fashion, she was unmistakenly a disturbingly attractive person."[7]

Belle pleaded, "Take this, read it, revise it, publish it, or burn it. Do what you will. It is the story of my adventures, misfortunes, imprisonments, and persecution."

After Belle's departure from his office, Sala found it difficult to transfer his thoughts from the charming lady and her predicament to the merits of her story. At the age of twenty-one, most lives are yet to be lived; yet, here was a young lady who had already crowded a lifetime into twenty-one years![8]

As he began to read the words of her manuscript, his interest quickened. Soon he was completely absorbed in the thrilling narrative and decided to publish it as written. *Belle Boyd in Camp and Prison* appeared in London in May 1865, published by Saunders, Otley, & Co. in a two-volume edition. It had very favorable reviews in the English press, and the English edition was quickly followed by one in America, a single volume published by Blelock & Co. of New York. (Both of these editions are now out of print; an original copy of each is in the Library of Congress in Washington.)[9]

Belle's own narrative, written hurriedly, is highly dramatic. She provided evidence for the truth of her story by giving names of officers, which makes it easy to verify her saga by tracing the army and navy records. Not one officer ever challenged her statements, and the accuracy of her story is supported by the memoirs, books, and papers of her contemporaries.

George Sala was completely captivated by Belle. Not only did he decide to publish her book, but he appealed to her admirers for immediate financial relief. The sight of her flowing eyes "that for 13 long months had refused to weep in a Northern prison," inspired him to write "A Word to Southern Sympathizers," which was published in *Morning Herald* of London, a paper consistently supportive of the Southern cause.[10]

He reminded his readers of their interest and excitement over the recent romantic wedding of Belle Boyd, of the return of her husband to the United States and to prison, of her present hard circumstances, and ended with an appeal for help. Immediate offers of assistance resulted; Belle was embarrassed but grateful, and wrote her appreciation to "the noblest and most hospitable people in the world."[11]

However, the income from her book could be only a temporary financial resource. For a young woman in a foreign land, soon to have a child to rear, some permanent occupation was necessary. What should it be? It occurred to her that she might try acting, dramatizing her own story. The attention she had received in the press abroad and at home, and the publication of her book, would pave the way.[12]

Again she sought the advice of Sala who had excellent connections in the literary and dramatic worlds. He knew not only writers but producers and actors, and encouraged Belle in her dramatic training and in her stage career. Coached by the English Shakespearean actor, Walter Montgomery, she made her debut at the Theatre Royale in Manchester in June 1866. She played the leading female role in Edward Bulwer-Lytton's play, *The Lady of Lyons*.[13]

Two other notable events happened that year. One was the birth of a daughter whom she named Grace. The other was the Proclamation of Amnesty issued by President Andrew Johnson which made it possible for her to go home again. At the end of 1866, Belle and her daughter returned to her native land, where she faced a new, very different life.[14] She was a mother, widow, author, and actress. What did the future hold?

Epilogue

JANUARY 1867—13 JUNE 1900

All the world's a stage,
And all the men and women merely players:
—William Shakespeare,
As You Like It, II.VII.139

BELLE PLANNED TO CONTINUE her theatrical career in her own country, making her first appearance on the American stage in St. Louis. Encouraged by her success there, she joined a theatre group and toured the South and Southwest. For this swing around the circuit, the group had as their manager John P. Smith of Richmond.[1]

In 1868, Belle played in New York City. She soon joined the Miles and Bates Stock Company in Cincinnati and assumed the stage name of Nina Benjamin. Later she played in theaters in Galveston and Houston, and then went to Louisiana where she performed at the New Orleans Theatre.[2]

At New Orleans she gave her last performance and retired from the stage at the age of twenty-five. She was being courted by an ardent admirer, John Swainston Hammond, a former British army officer. He came to the United States in the early stages of the Civil War and served in the Union Army as a first lieutenant in the Seventh Massachusetts Infantry. He visited New Orleans, and while there, attended a performance at the New Orleans Theatre. He was so fascinated by Nina Benjamin that he sought a mutual acquaintance and arranged a meeting.[3]

They were married there in March 1869. At the time of his marriage, Hammond was a prosperous businessman who traveled extensively as a sales representative in the tea and coffee business. After their marriage, the Hammonds moved to California. A son was born; he died in his first or second year.[4]

The Hammonds lived in various places in the United States as required by his business. They were active in social and community activities wherever they lived. Three other children (two daughters and a son) were born. Belle's cousin, Sue Boyd Barton, mentions that Hammond was entertained in the Barton home in Knoxville.[5]

On 3 May 1880, Belle's mother died at the home of her son-in-law, O. W. Rowland, near Charles Town, West Virginia. Perhaps fifty-four years old, she is said to have died from stomach cancer. She was buried beside her husband in the Green Hill Cemetery in Martinsburg. Of her burial a local Martinsburg paper observed: "Among others accompanying the remains was the celebrated Belle Boyd, daughter of the deceased. It was her first visit for years to the scenes of her childhood and of the daring exploits of her girlhood during the war. The circumstances of her visit were extremely sad."[6]

For almost sixteen years the Hammonds led a seemingly happy life. However, serious difficulty arose and they were divorced in 1884, with Belle receiving a substantial financial settlement. He created trust funds for his children to provide for their education.[7]

In 1885, at forty-one years of age, Belle married again, this time to Nathaniel Rue High, son of the Reverend Nathaniel High of Toledo, Ohio. He was younger than Belle, but that only matched her youthful spirit. As an actor, his income was not sufficient to support a wife and four children, so Belle decided to tour the country, giving dramatic recitals. Her husband became her business and stage manager.

She gave monologues relating her experiences as a Confederate agent and had much dramatic appeal in both North and South. She usually concluded by stressing the unity of the nation with the stirring words, "One God, One Flag, One People Forever." For the veterans of both North and South she became "Our Belle." She continued these recitals for some fourteen years, taking the children with her and giving them professional training and stage experience.[8]

Belle arrived in Kilbourn, Wisconsin (now Wisconsin Dells) on 9 June 1900. She was to give a recital on 13 June, but on that evening she suffered a severe heart attack. She died before a physician could arrive. She was fifty-six years old, but looked much younger.

Her husband called the children to Kilbourn, where funeral services were held in the Episcopal Church and she was buried in the local cemetery. Four veterans from the Union Army and two from the Spanish American War lowered the remains of the Rebel Spy into her grave, and a simple marker was emplaced.

In 1919, a Confederate veteran (Third Missouri Regiment) from Greenville, Mississippi, Private Willis A. Everman (unrelated to Belle), had a small granite tombstone erected:

BELLE BOYD

Confederate Spy

Born in Virginia

Died in Wisconsin

Erected by a Comrade[9]

notes

The chief source used was Belle's own story, *Belle Boyd in Camp and Prison*. There are two editions of her book: the two-volume English edition, published in London in 1865, and the single-volume American edition published in New York in 1865 and 1867. The contents of the two editions are the same; the type of the English edition is larger, necessitating two volumes, and consequently the page numbers differ. The version used here is the American edition. A second major source was Louis A. Sigaud's definitive biography, *Belle Boyd, Confederate Spy*. Another valuable reference and source of background was Curtis Carroll Davis's annotated edition of Belle's work.

For general background on the war (battles, military maneuvers, campaigns, etc.) I have cited various American history texts.

Chapter 1
(Based on Belle Boyd, *Belle Boyd in Camp and Prison*,
New York: Blelock and Co., 1865, 1867, pp. 45-52.)

1. Boyd, p. 50.

2. F. V. Aler, *Aler's History of Martinsburg and Berkeley County* [WV], chapters 6, 9, and 10.

3. The Boyd family Bible entry shows 9 May 1843, but Belle and her family insist on 1844. At the age of twelve she went to Mount Washington Female College in Baltimore, which had no students prior to May 1856. To assert that she was born in 1843 is to maintain that she was twelve in 1855 and attended a school that was not founded until the next year. As for official birth records, there are none for Martinsburg prior to 1865. Bernard C. Steiner, *History of Education in Maryland*; Louis A. Sigaud, *Belle Boyd, Confederate Spy*, p. 224.

4. Sigaud, p. 5.

5. Millard K. Bushong, *History of Jefferson County, West Virginia*, p. 305; A. D. Kenamond [article on Glenn Burnie] pp. 13-25.

6. The oldest child died in infancy and is buried at Glenn Burnie.

7. Sigaud, pp. 9-11.

8. Ibid., pp. 2-3.

9. Boyd, p. 47.

10. Aler, *History of Martinsburg*, chapters 6, 9, and 10.

11. The house at 126 E. Burke Street was later razed to make room for another building, noted in the *Martinsburg Journal*, 23 August 1957, with an illustration above the heading "One of Community's Oldest Buildings Is Now in Process of Being Torn Down." Curtis Carroll Davis, *Belle Boyd in Camp and Prison*, p. 362.

12. Boyd, pp. 48-49, 57.

13. Ibid., pp. 73-75.

14. Ibid., p. 49.

15. Sigaud, p. 3, and Boyd, pp. 49-50.

16. Sigaud, p. 28.

17. Ibid., p. 1.

18. Boyd, p. 45.

19. James Ford Rhodes, *History of the United States*, vol. 1, pp. 10-13.

20. Ibid., p. 12.

21. Sources on slavery: William E. Dodd, *The Cotton Kingdom—A Chronicle of the Old South*, pp. 48-70; Frank L. Owsley, *King Cotton Diplomacy—Foreign Relations of the Confederate States of America*, pp. 50-51.

22. Sigaud, p. 17.

23. Boyd, p. 50.

24. Sigaud, p. 4.

25. Steiner, *Education in Maryland*, p. 270. This school was attended by Mary Ella MacDonald of Martinsburg, who one day was taken by the Dean to the Octagon Room and shown Belle's initials, cut in one of the windows—Mary Ella MacDonald, [article on Belle Boyd]; [Boyd, Belle, at Mt. Washington College] [a newspaper article]. For details about the school, see B. Latrobe Weston, "The Story of Mt. Washington, Maryland."

26. Sigaud, p. 4.

27. James Ford Rhodes, *History of the United States*, vol. 2, pp. 251-61.

28. Ibid., pp. 321-41.

29. Steiner, *Education in Maryland*, pp. 270-71.

30. Ibid., pp. 270-73.

31. Boyd, p. 54.

32. Rhodes, *History of U.S.*, vol. 2, pp. 383-85, 391-96.

33. Boyd, pp. 50-51.

34. Sigaud, p. 22.

35. Boyd, p. 51.

36. Ibid., pp. 50-51.

37. Ibid.

38. Sigaud, pp. 96-97.

39. Boyd, p. 50.

40. "John Brown's Body . . ." originated in the spring of 1861 when the words were composed by members of the Daniel Webster Regiment of Massachusetts and set to the music of the hymn, "Glory, Glory, Hallelujah." Rhodes, *History of U.S.*, vol. 2, pp. 401-409, 415-16.

41. Ibid., pp. 501-502.

42. Boyd, p. 57.

Chapter 2
(Based on Belle Boyd, *Belle Boyd in Camp and Prison*, pp. 53-67.)

1. Boyd, pp. 65-66.

2. James Ford Rhodes, *History of the U.S.*, vol.1, pp. 385-87.

3. E. M. Coulter, *The Confederate States of America, 1861-65: History of the South*, Volume 7, p. 74.

4. Rhodes, *History of the U.S.*, vol. 3, pp. 365-66.

5. F. V. Aler, *Aler's History of Martinsburg and Berkeley County*, p. 228. Speaking of the number of prominent Virginians who joined the Stonewall Brigade, "so also did the father of the Confederacy's best-known female spy, Belle Boyd." Also in James I. Robertson, Jr., *The Stonewall Brigade*, p. 19.

6. Boyd, pp. 56-57.

7. John Esten Cooke, *The Wearing of the Gray*, p. 371.

8. Henry Kyd Douglas, *I Rode With Stonewall*, p. 55.

9. Coulter, *Confederate States*, p. 415.

10. Louis A. Sigaud, *Belle Boyd, Confederate Spy*, pp. 6-7.

11. Myrta Lockett Avary, *A Virginia Girl in the Civil War, 1861-1865*, chapter 5.

12. John Bakeless, *Spies of the Confederacy*, pp. 141-42.

13. Sigaud, pp. 8-9.

14. Ibid., pp. 74, 76, 84.

15. O. Frederick Morton, *The History of Winchester in Virginia*, p. 188.

16. Boyd, p. 57.

17. Douglas, *Stonewall*, p. 6.

18. Boyd, p. 59.

19. Rhodes, *History of the U.S.*, vol. 2, pp. 384-85; Boyd, p. 59.

20. Boyd, p. 60.

21. Ibid., pp. 61-62.

22. Douglas, *Stonewall*, p. 6.

23. Boyd, pp. 62-63.

24. Ibid., pp. 62-65.

25. Morton, *Winchester*, pp. 148-49.

26. Boyd, pp. 65-66.

27. Ibid., pp. 66-67.

Chapter 3

(Based on Belle Boyd, *Belle Boyd in Camp and Prison*, pp. 68-78.)

1. Boyd, p. 75.

2. Ibid., pp. 68-70.

3. Ibid., p. 73.

4. These sources discuss the shooting of the Yankee and his burial in Martinsburg: John Bakeless, *Spies of the Confederacy*, p. 145; Samuel P. Bates, *History of Pennsylvania Volunteers, 1861-65*, p. 76; and Louis A. Sigaud, *Belle Boyd, Confederate Spy*, p. 15.

5. Boyd, p. 73.

6. Ibid., p. 72.

7. Ibid., pp. 74-75.

8. Ibid., p. 75.

9. Boyd, p. 74.

10. Sigaud, p. 16.

11. U.S. War Department, *The War of the Rebellion: A Compilation of the Official Records of the Union and Confederate Armies*, series 2, vol. 2, p. 561.

12. Boyd, p. 74.

13. Ibid., p. 76; Sigaud, p. 17.

14. Boyd, p. 76.

15. Ibid., p. 77.

16. Ibid., pp. 77-78.

17. Ibid., p. 78.

18. Ibid., p. 80.

Chapter 4

(Based on Belle Boyd, *Belle Boyd in Camp and Prison*, pp. 79-92.)

1. Boyd, p. 82.

2. Ralph Harlow, *The Growth of the United States*, p. 482.

3. James Ford Rhodes, *History of the U.S.*, vol. 3, p. 411.

4. Harlow, *Growth*, p. 483.

5. Ibid.

6. James I. Robertson, Jr., *The Stonewall Brigade*, pp. 37-44. For a good account of the battle of Manassas, see Samuel Eliot Morrison and Henry Steele Commager, *The Growth of the American Republic*, vol. 1, pp. 699-702.

7. Ibid.

8. E. M. Coulter, *The Confederate States of America, 1861-65*, p. 344.

9. Mary Boykin Chestnut, *A Diary from Dixie*, p. 99.

10. Boyd, p. 80.

11. Ibid., p. 82.

12. Ibid.

13. Ibid., p. 91.

14. Ibid., pp. 91-92.

15. Ibid., pp. 82-83.

16. Ibid., p. 57.

17. Louis A. Sigaud, *Belle Boyd, Confederate Spy*, p. 24.

18. Harry Gilmor, *Four Years in the Saddle*, p. 73.

19. Boyd, p. 83.

20. Sigaud, p. 28.

21. Ibid., p. 25.

22. Louis A. Sigaud, "More About Belle Boyd," p. 177.

23. Boyd, p. 78.

Chapter 5

(Based on Belle Boyd, *Belle Boyd in Camp and Prison*, pp. 83-93.)

1. Boyd, p. 85.

2. Ibid., p. 83.

3. Sigaud, *Belle Boyd, Confederate Spy*, p. 28.

4. Boyd, pp. 84-85.

5. Ibid., pp. 85-86.

6. Ibid., p. 86.

7. Ibid., p. 87.

8. Ibid., pp. 87-88.

9. E. M. Coulter, *The Confederate States of America, 1861-65*, p. 341.

10. James Ford Rhodes, *History of the U.S.*, pp. 462-63.

11. Coulter, *Confederate States*, pp. 354-55. A description of the Peninsula campaign can be found in Rhodes, *History of the U.S.*, pp. 490-96.

Chapter 6

(Based on Belle Boyd, *Belle Boyd in Camp and Prison*, pp. 93-116.)

1. Boyd, p. 98.

2. Ibid., p. 94.

3. Ibid.

4. Ibid.; Louis A. Sigaud, *Belle Boyd, Confederate Spy*, p. 30.

5. Boyd, p. 95.

6. Ibid.

7. Ibid., p. 96.

8. Ibid., p. 97.

9. Ibid., pp. 98-99.

10. Ibid.

11. Sigaud, p. 32.

12. Boyd, p. 100.

13. Ibid., pp. 100-101.

14. The Belle Boyd Cottage, in the Strickler House yard at Front Royal, is illustrated in Laura Virginia Hale, *Belle Boyd, Southern Spy of the Shenandoah*. The cottage still stands immediately to the rear of, and partly attached to, the commercial establishment erected on the site of the hotel. The cottage is now a clothing store owned by Edward Stokes, proprietor of the Stokes Furniture Company across the street. He also owns the building in front of the cottage on the site of the old Strickler House. (Note: The cottage was moved to Front Royal's Historic District in 1982.)

15. Boyd, p. 101.

16. Ibid., pp. 101-102.

17. David Hunter Strother, *A Virginia Yankee in the Civil War*, entry of 19 May 1862.

Chapter 7

(Based on Belle Boyd, *Belle Boyd in Camp and Prison*, pp. 103-16; Thomas A. Ashby, *Life of Turner Ashby*, pp. 164-65; Douglas Southall Freeman, *Lee's Lieutenants*, pp. 371-72.)

1. Boyd, pp. 102-103.

2. "Captain K," as Belle calls him, was identified as Captain (later Brigadier General) Daniel J. Keily, an aide to General Shields, by Louis A. Sigaud (*Belle Boyd, Confederate Spy*, pp. 60-61).

3. Boyd, pp. 103-104.

4. Ibid., pp. 104-105. An example of the type of cipher Belle probably employed (the "double key" method) is provided in Sigaud, pp. 228-30.

5. Boyd, p. 104.

6. Freeman, *Lee's Lieutenants*, pp. 371-72.

7. Boyd, p. 104.

8. Ibid., pp. 105-106.

9. Ibid.

10. Ibid., p. 107.

11. For an analysis of the Confederate strategy in the 1862 campaign, see Millard K. Bushong, "Jackson in the Shenandoah", pp. 85-96.

12. Curtis Carroll Davis, *Belle Boyd in Camp and Prison*, p. 368.

13. Sigaud, pp. 60-61.

14. U. S. War Department, *Official Records of the Union and Confederate Armies*, series 1, vol. 12, pp. 690, 697.

Chapter 8
(Based on Belle Boyd, *Belle Boyd in Camp and Prison*, pp. 93-116.)

1. Boyd, pp. 108-109.

2. Ibid., p. 107.

3. Louis A. Sigaud, *Belle Boyd, Confederate Spy*, p. 9.

4. Lucy Rebecca Buck, Diary, 1861-1865, entry of 14 May 1862.

5. Ibid.

6. Boyd, p. 108.

7. Ibid., p. 109.

8. Buck, Diary, entry of 21 May 1862.

9. Sigaud, p. 40.

10. The "gentleman of high social position" who gave the letters to Belle is identified by Louis Sigaud as Colonel William R. Denny of Winchester, Virginia. He was a member of the 31st militia who, because of serious illness, had been sent home to recuperate after being captured by the Federals; while at home he acted as a gatherer of information. This was revealed in a letter dated 28 March 1963 from Colonel Sigaud to Mr. and Mrs. George Evans of Bruceton Mills, West Virginia. The letter is now in the collection of the Blennerhassett Island Historical Park Museum in Parkersburg WV.

11. Boyd, p. 110.

12. Sigaud, p. 43.

13. Boyd, p. 110.

14. Ibid., pp. 111-12.

15. Ibid., pp. 112-13; Sigaud, p. 41.

16. Boyd, pp. 113-16.

17. Ibid., p. 115.

18. Sigaud, pp. 43, 44, 172.

Chapter 9
(Based on Belle Boyd, *Belle Boyd in Camp and Prison*, pp. 117-33. An excellent account of Belle's role in the Battle of Front Royal is in L. V. Hale, *Four Valiant Years*,

pp. 140-41. Perhaps the most exciting general account of the battle is by General Richard Taylor, son of former President Zachary Taylor, in *Destruction and Reconstruction*, pp. 53-54. Another dramatic account is by Henry Kyd Douglas in *I Rode With Stonewall*, pp. 51-52.)

1. Douglas, *Stonewall*, pp. 51-52.

2. Taylor, *Destruction and Reconstruction*, p. 52.

3. Boyd, pp. 117-18.

4. Ibid., pp. 122-23.

5. Ibid., p. 118.

6. Ibid., p. 119.

7. Ibid., pp. 119-20.

8. Ibid.

9. Ibid., p. 125.

10. Ibid., pp. 125-26.

11. Ibid., p. 127.

12. Ibid.; Douglas, *Stonewall*, p. 51; Lenoir Chambers, *Stonewall Jackson*, pp. 524-25.

13. Taylor, *Destruction and Reconstruction*, pp. 51-52.

14. Boyd, p. 128.

15. Douglas, *Stonewall*, pp. 51-52.

16. Boyd, pp. 128-29; Louis A. Sigaud, *Belle Boyd, Confederate Spy*, pp. 49-50.

17. Boyd, p. 133.

18. Sigaud, pp. 211-12.

19. Sigaud, p. 56.

20. Boyd, p. 132.

21. Sigaud, p. 57.

22. Boyd, p. 130.

23. Ibid., pp. 132-33.

Chapter 10
(Based on Belle Boyd, *Belle Boyd in Camp and Prison*, pp. 131-44.)

1. Boyd, p. 140.

2. Ibid., p. 131.

3. Ibid., p. 134.

4. Ibid., pp. 134-38.

5. Louis A. Sigaud, *Belle Boyd, Confederate Spy*, p. 62; Boyd, p. 138.

6. In Belle's book, "Maginnis" is spelled "McEnnis." The misspelling was discovered by Maginnis's daughter, Mrs. J. M. Cannock of Germantown, PA, and mentioned in a letter of 18 January 1946 to Louis Sigaud. The letter was found among

Sigaud's notes, which he had intended to use in a later edition of his book, *Belle Boyd, Confederate Spy*. Sigaud's explanation to Mrs. Cannock in a letter of 25 January 1946, is that Belle spelled the name as she pronounced it. (These notes are in the museum operated by the Blennerhassett Island Historical Park Commission, Parkersburg, WV.)

7. Boyd, p. 139; Sigaud, p. 62.

8. Boyd, p. 140.

9. Ibid., p. 141.

10. Ibid., p. 142.

11. Sigaud, pp. 63-64.

12. Boyd, p. 143; Sigaud, pp. 63-64.

13. Boyd, pp. 143-44.

Chapter 11

(Based on Belle Boyd, *Belle Boyd in Camp and Prison*, pp. 145-85.)

1. Catherine M. Jones, *Heroines of Dixie*, p. 173. Interesting biographical sketches of Southern women in the war.

2. Boyd, pp. 146-48.

3. Ibid., p. 149.

4. U. S. War Department, *Official Records of the Union and Confederate Armies*, series 2, vol. 4, p. 310.

5. Boyd, p. 151.

6. Ibid., pp. 151-53.

7. Ibid., pp. 153-55.

8. Lucy Rebecca Buck, Diary, 1861-1865, entry of 30 July 1862.

9. Boyd, p. 157.

10. Ibid., p. 157.

11. Louis A. Sigaud, *Belle Boyd, Confederate Spy*, p. 70.

12. Boyd, pp. 157-59.

13. U. S. War Department, *Records*, series 2, vol. 4, pp. 309-10.

14. Boyd, pp. 160-61.

15. Ibid., pp. 165-66; Sigaud, p. 72.

16. Boyd, pp. 166-72; Sigaud, p. 73.

17. Boyd, pp. 174-75.

Chapter 12

(Based on Belle Boyd, *Belle Boyd in Camp and Prison*, pp. 164-202.)

1. Richard Lovelace, *To Althea, From Prison*, stanza 4.

2. Louis A. Sigaud, *Belle Boyd, Confederate Spy*, p. 77.

3. Ibid.

4. Ibid., pp. 77-78.

5. William E. Doster, *Lincoln and Episodes of the Civil War*, p. 105.

6. Boyd, p. 177.

7. Doster, *Episodes*, pp. 104-105.

8. Ibid., pp. 101-102.

9. Boyd, p. 177.

10. *Boyd's Washington and Georgetown Directory* for 1858 and 1860 lists Floyd's residence at 345 I Street, North, according to Curtis Carroll Davis, *Belle Boyd in Camp and Prison*, p. 375.

11. Boyd, p. 178.

12. Ibid., p. 181.

13. Ibid., pp. 181-83.

14. Ibid., p. 177.

15. Ibid., p. 184.

Chapter 13

(Based on Belle Boyd, *Belle Boyd in Camp and Prison*, pp. 185-202.)

1. James J. Williamson, *Prison Life in the Old Capitol*, pp. 50-51.

2. Boyd, pp. 189-90.

3. Louis A. Sigaud, *Belle Boyd, Confederate Spy*, p. 77.

4. Boyd, p. 187.

5. Ibid., p. 188.

6. William E. Doster, *Lincoln and Episodes of the Civil War*, p. 103.

7. M. P. Andrews, *Women of the South in War Times*, p. 66. The words to "Maryland, My Maryland" were adapted by the Cary sisters to the music of Lauringer Horatius.

8. Curtis Carroll Davis, *Belle Boyd in Camp and Prison*, p. 75.

9. Williamson, *Prison Life*, pp. 50-51.

10. Ibid.

11. Boyd, pp. 196-97.

12. Sigaud, p. 88.

13. Boyd, p. 194.

14. Ibid., pp. 194-95.

15. Sigaud, p. 90.

16. Dennis A. Mahony, *The Prisoner of State*, pp. 268-69.

17. Boyd, pp. 198-200.

18. Sigaud, p. 86.

19. U. S. War Department, *Official Records of the Union and Confederate Armies*, series 2, vol. 4, p. 349.

20. Ibid.

21. Joseph O. Kerbey, *The Boy Spy*, pp. 412-30.

22. Ibid.

23. Sigaud, pp. 96-97.

24. Doster, *Episodes*, pp. 102-103.

25. Sigaud, pp. 96-97.

26. Mahony, *Prisoner of State*, pp. 268-69.

27. Boyd, p. 202.

Chapter 14

(Based on Belle Boyd, *Belle Boyd in Camp and Prison*, pp. 197-206.)

1. James J. Williamson, *Prison Life in the Old Capitol*, p. 51.

2. Boyd, p. 197.

3. U. S. War Department, *Official Records of the Union and Confederate Armies*, series 2, vol. 4, p. 461.

4. Ibid.

5. Boyd, p. 198.

6. Dennis A. Mahony, *The Prisoner of State*, p. 270.

7. Louis A. Sigaud, *Belle Boyd, Confederate Spy*, pp. 98, 112.

8. Carl Sandburg, *Abraham Lincoln, The War Years*, p. 504.

9. Boyd, pp. 203-204.

10. Ibid., pp. 204-205.

11. Ibid., p. 205; Sigaud, p. 102.

12. Sigaud, pp. 96-97, 112.

Chapter 15

(Based on Belle Boyd, *Belle Boyd in Camp and Prison*, pp. 203-22.)

1. Boyd, p. 208.

2. Ibid., pp. 205-206.

3. Ibid., p. 207.

4. Ibid., pp. 205-207.

5. Ibid., p. 207.

6. Ibid.; Louis A. Sigaud, *Belle Boyd, Confederate Spy*, pp. 103-104.

7. Boyd, pp. 207-208.

8. Samuel Eliot Morrison and Henry Steele Commager, *The Growth of the American Republic*, vol. 1, p. 734; Richard N. Current, T. Harry Williams, and Frank Friedel, *American History: A Survey*, Vol. 7, p. 380.

9. Boyd, p. 208; Sigaud, p. 104.

10. Boyd, p. 210; Sigaud, p. 107; Sue Boyd Barton, letter to Mary Nelson.

11. Sigaud, p. 199.

12. Myrta Lockett Avary, *A Virginia Girl in the Civil War*, ch. 5.

13. Boyd, pp. 210-11; Current and others, *American History*, vol. 1, p. 394.

14. Ibid., p. 213.

Chapter 16

(Based on Belle Boyd, *Belle Boyd in Camp and Prison*, pp. 203-22; and Myrta Lockett Avary, *A Virginia Girl in the Civil War, 1861-1865*.)

1. Avary, p. 58.

2. James Truslow Adams, *America's Tragedy*, pp. 241-47.

3. Curtis Carroll Davis, *Belle Boyd in Camp and Prison*, p. 78.

4. Avary, pp. 51-58.

5. Sigaud, p. 15, and Boyd, pp. 213-14.

6. Oliver P. Chitwood, R. W. Patrick, and Frank L. Owsley, *The American People, A History*, vol. 1, pp. 468-69.

7. Boyd, p. 215, and Sigaud, pp. 115-16.

8. Boyd, p. 214, and Sigaud, pp. 115-16.

9. Boyd, pp. 214-15.

10. Sue Boyd Barton, letter to Mary Nelson, 11 March 1932.

Chapter 17

(Based on Belle Boyd, *Belle Boyd in Camp and Prison*, pp. 203-22.)

1. Boyd, p. 217.

2. Ibid., p. 216.

3. Ibid., p. 217.

4. Ibid.

5. Allen Johnson and Dumas Malone, eds., *Dictionary of American Biography*, vol. 2, pp. 111-12.

6. Richard N. Current, T. Harry Williams, and Frank Friedel, *American History: A Survey*, vol. 7, p. 379.

7. Ibid., pp. 386-88.

8. Harry Gilmor, *Four Years in the Saddle*, pp. 73-74.

9. Boyd, pp. 219-20.

10. Ibid., pp. 221-22.

11. Ibid., p. 400.

12. Ibid., p. 222.

Chapter 18
(Based on Belle Boyd, *Belle Boyd in Camp and Prison*, pp. 223-37.)

1. Boyd, p. 227.

2. James G. Randall and David Donald, *The Civil War and Reconstruction*, pp. 236-42, and Charles H. Ambler and F. P. Summers, *West Virginia, the Mountain State*, pp. 145-205 and 239-47, provided general background for this chapter.

3. Randall and Donald, *Civil War*, p. 241.

4. A detailed description of the Battle of Gettysburg is given in Bruce Catton, *Glory Road*, pp. 268-322.

5. Richard N. Current, T. Harry Williams, and Frank Freidel, *American History: A Survey*, p. 396.

6. Ibid.

7. E. M. Coulter, *The Confederate States of America, 1861-65*, pp. 357-58.

8. Current, Williams, and Freidel, *History*, p. 396.

9. Boyd, pp. 224-25.

10. Ibid.

11. Ibid., pp. 226-27.

12. Ibid., p. 228.

13. Ibid., pp. 228-29.

14. James Hunter Stevenson, *Boots and Saddles*, pp. 219-25.

15. Louis A. Sigaud, "More About Belle Boyd", p. 176.

16. Boyd, p. 230.

Chapter 19
(Based on Belle Boyd, *Belle Boyd in Camp and Prison*, pp. 222-54.)

1. Boyd, p. 231.

2. Ibid.

3. Ibid., p. 234.

4. Ibid., p. 232.

5. Ibid.

6. Ibid., pp. 234-37.

7. Louis A. Sigaud, *Belle Boyd, Confederate Spy*, p. 127.

8. George A. Lawrence, *Border and Bastille*, pp. 195-96.

9. Boyd, p. 238.

10. Sigaud, p. 130.

11. Boyd, pp. 242-43.

12. Curtis Carroll Davis, *Belle Boyd in Camp and Prison*, pp. 386-87.

13. Sigaud, p. 132, and Boyd, p. 245. The career of Annie Jones is summarized in Mary E. Massey, *Bonnet Brigades*, pp. 73-76.

14. Boyd, p. 247.

15. Mr. Boyd and Lamon had known each other since boyhood, as both lived in Berkeley County VA. Lamon studied law in Louisville, Kentucky, then moved to Danville, Illinois. In 1852 he became the Danville law partner of Lincoln. Campaigning for Lincoln in 1860, he accompanied the President-elect to Washington in February 1861, being personally responsible for Lincoln's safety. In April 1861 Lincoln appointed him marshal of the District of Columbia.—Allen Johnson, ed., *Dictionary of American Biography*, pp. 562-63.

16. Sigaud, p. 139.

17. Boyd, pp. 253-54.

18. Ibid.

19. Sigaud, p. 81.

20. Boyd, p. 260.

21. Ibid., p. 248, and Sigaud, p. 136.

22. Boyd, pp. 249-51.

23. Ibid., p. 254.

Chapter 20

(Based on Belle Boyd, *Belle Boyd in Camp and Prison*, pp. 255-68.)

1. Boyd, p. 257.

2. Ibid., pp. 248-49.

3. Ibid., pp. 255-56.

4. Ibid., pp. 256-57.

5. Louis A. Sigaud, *Belle Boyd, Confederate Spy*, p. 141.

6. E. M. Coulter, *The Confederate States of America, 1861-65*, p. 370.

7. F. L. Owsley, *King Cotton Diplomacy*, pp. 323-24.

8. Sigaud, p. 141.

9. Ibid., p. 142.

10. Edward A. Pollard, *Observations in the North*, p. 106.

11. Mary Boykin Chestnut, *A Diary from Dixie*, p. 165. For Butler's reaction to his interview with Belle, see Hans L. Trefousse, *Ben Butler—The South Called Him Beast*, pp. 144-45.

12. Sigaud, p. 141.

13. Boyd, pp. 257-59, and Sigaud, p. 142.

14. Boyd, p. 259, and Sigaud, p. 143.

15. Boyd, pp. 260-62.

16. Euphemia Goldsborough, Diary, 1861-1865, entry for 4 December 1863. Her diary, portable desk, and other possessions are owned by her granddaughter, Mrs. Stuart Crim of Summit Point, West Virginia.

17. Boyd, pp. 263-64.

18. Ibid., p. 264.

Chapter 21
(Based on Belle Boyd, *Belle Boyd in Camp and Prison*, pp. 264-76.)

1. Boyd, p. 274.

2. Ibid., pp. 269-73.

3. Ibid., p. 272.

4. Ibid., p. 273.

5. Quoted in Curtis Carroll Davis, *Belle Boyd in Camp and Prison*, p. 390.

6. Boyd, pp. 273-74.

7. E. M. Coulter, *The Confederate States of America, 1861-65*, p. 305.

8. Boyd, pp. 274-75.

9. Ibid., p. 275.

10. Louis A. Sigaud, "More About Belle Boyd," p. 175.

11. Boyd, pp. 275-76.

Chapter 22
(Belle's capture at sea is completely documented in U. S. Navy Department, *Official Records of the Union and Confederate Navies in the War of the Rebellion*. This chapter is based on Belle Boyd, *Belle Boyd in Camp and Prison*, pp. 275-91.)

1. Boyd, p. 279.

2. Richard N. Current, T. Harry Williams, and Frank Friedel, *American History: A Survey*, vol. 1, pp. 387-88.

3. For a good description of the blockade, see Samuel Eliot Morrison and Henry Steele Commager, *The Growth of the American Republic*, pp. 705-707.

4. Boyd, p. 276.

5. Edward A. Pollard, *Observations in the North*, p. 2.

6. U. S. Navy Department, *Official Records*, series 1 vol. 10, p. 42.

7. Ibid., 1:21:214.

8. Boyd, p. 277.

9. U. S. Navy Department, *Official Records*, series 1, vol. 2, p. 613, and series 1, vol. 9, p. 539.

10. Boyd, pp. 278-91.

11. U. S. Navy Department, *Official Records*, series 1, vol. 27, p. 687.

12. Ibid., 1:10:42.

Chapter 23
(Based on Belle Boyd, *Belle Boyd in Camp and Prison*, pp. 292-316.)

Chapter 24
(Based on Belle Boyd, *Belle Boyd in Camp and Prison*, pp. 311-29.)

1. Boyd, p. 313.

2. Edward A. Pollard, editor of the Richmond *Examiner*, was briefly imprisoned in Fort Warren, paroled, then placed in solitary confinement at Fortress Monroe on orders from Stanton. While there, for reasons unclear, the unpredictable Benjamin Butler sent him South in defiance of the order. In his book *Observations in the North*, Pollard denounces the taking of the *Greyhound* and his treatment. (Louis A. Sigaud, *Belle Boyd, Confederate Spy*, pp. 152-53.)

Chapter 25
(Based on Belle Boyd, *Belle Boyd in Camp and Prison*, pp. 330-40.)

1. Boyd, p. 331.

2. Louis A. Sigaud, *Belle Boyd, Confederate Spy*, p. 170.

3. Boyd, p. 27.

4. Ibid., pp. 335-36.

Chapter 26
(Based on Belle Boyd, *Belle Boyd in Camp and Prison*, pp. 330-40.)

1. John Milton, *Paradise Lost*, Book 4, lines 750-51.

2. Louis A. Sigaud, *Belle Boyd, Confederate Spy*, p. 176.

3. Boyd, pp. 338-40.

4. Ibid., p. 336.

5. Sigaud, p. 176.

6. Boyd, p. 464.

7. Belle's letter to Davis is in the Confederate Records, National Archives, in Washington. The letter is printed in Louis A. Sigaud, "William Boyd Compton: Belle Boyd's Cousin," pp. 22-33.

Chapter 27
(Based on Belle Boyd, *Belle Boyd in Camp and Prison*, "Samuel Hardinge's Journal," pp. 341-434.)

1. Boyd, p. 346.

2. Ibid., pp. 345-46.

3. Ibid., pp. 347, 355-56.

4. Ibid., p. 371.

5. Ibid., p. 383.

6. Ibid., pp. 396-97, and Louis A. Sigaud, *Belle Boyd, Confederate Spy*, pp. 181-82.

7. Boyd, pp. 451-56.

8. Margaret Leech, *Reveille in Washington, 1860-1865*, p. 432.

9. Sue Boyd Barton, letter to Mary Nelson, 11 March 1932.

10. Boyd, p. 21.

11. Curtis Carroll Davis, *Belle Boyd in Camp and Prison*, p. 17.

Chapter 28

1. Louis A. Sigaud, "When Belle Boyd Wrote Lincoln," pp. 15-22.

2. Ibid., p. 20.

3. Boyd, pp. 384-85.

4. Ibid., p. 449.

5. Sigaud, p. 20.

6. Boyd, pp. 27-28.

7. Ibid., pp. 458-63.

Chapter 29

1. Boyd, p. 14.

2. Ibid., p. 17.

3. A vivid description of Lee's surrender is in Bruce Catton, *A Stillness at Appomattox*, pp. 368-80.

4. Boyd, p. 13.

5. Ibid., p. 21.

6. Ibid., p. 14.

7. Louis A. Sigaud, *Belle Boyd, Confederate Spy*, p. vii.

8. Boyd, p. 14.

9. Sigaud, pp. 185-86. Both editions were carefully studied by the author in writing this book.

10. Boyd, pp. 16-19.

11. Ibid., pp. 21-22.

12. Sigaud, p. 186.

13. Ibid., p. 187.

14. Ibid.

Chapter 30

1. Curtis Carroll Davis, *Belle Boyd in Camp and Prison*, p. 19.

2. Ibid., pp. 21-22.

3. Ibid., pp. 22-23, and Louis Sigaud, *Belle Boyd, Confederate Spy*, p. 191.

4. Davis, p. 23, and Sigaud, pp. 192-93.

5. Sue Boyd Barton, letter to Mary Nelson, 11 March 1932.

6. *Charles Town Spirit of Jefferson*, 11 May 1880.

7. Davis, pp. 22-25, and Sigaud, pp. 191-94.

8. Davis, pp. 28-30, and Sigaud, pp. 195-97.

9. Davis, pp. 33-36, and Sigaud, pp. 200-201.

Bibliography

Adams, James Truslow. *America's Tragedy*. New York: Charles Scribner's Sons, 1934.

Aler, F. V. *Aler's History of Martinsburg and Berkeley County (WV)*. Hagerstown MD: The Mail Publishing Co., 1888.

Ambler, Charles H., and F. P. Summers. *West Virginia, the Mountain State*. Second edition. Englewood Cliffs NJ: Prentice-Hall, 1958.

Andrews, M. P. *Women of the South in War Times*. Baltimore: The Norman Remington Co., 1924.

Ashby, Thomas A. *The Valley Campaigns*. New York: Neale Publishing Co., 1914.

———. *Life of Turner Ashby*. New York: Neale Publishing Co., 1914.

Avary, Myrta Lockett. *A Virginia Girl in the Civil War, 1861-1865: Being A Record of the Actual Experiences of the Wife of A Confederate Officer*. New York: D. Appleton and Co., 1903.

Bakeless, John. *Spies of the Confederacy*. New York: J. B. Lippincott Co., 1970.

Barton, Sue Boyd. Letter to Mary Nelson, 11 March 1932. Knoxville TN: Lawson McGhee Library, McClung Historical Room, Belle Boyd Collection.

Bassett, John Spencer. *A Short History of the U. S.* New York: Macmillan Co., 1923.

Bates, Samuel P. *History of the Pennsylvania Volunteers, 1861-65*. Harrisburg PA: B. Singerley, 1869-1871.

Boyd, Belle. *Belle Boyd in Camp and Prison*. Two volumes. London: Saunders, Otley, and Co., 1865.

_____ . *Belle Boyd in Camp and Prison*. New York: Blelock and Co., 1865, 1867. (Official) "diary" of Belle Boyd; edition used for the present work.)

[Boyd, Belle, at Mt. Washington College.] *Martinsburg (WV) Evening Journal*, 16 July 1979.

[Boyd, Mary, death of.] *Charleston* [WV] *Spirit of Jefferson*, 11 May 1880.

[Boyd, Mary, death of.] *Martinsburg* [WV] *Independent*, 8 May 1880.

Boyd, William P. *History of the Boyd Family and Descendants*. Rochester NY: John P. Smith Printing Co., 1912.

Buck, Lucy Rebecca. Diary, 1861-1865. Front Royal VA: Samuels Library. Mimeographed, copyrighted 1940.

Bushong, Millard K. *History of Jefferson County, West Virginia*. Charles Town WV: Jefferson Publishing Co., 1941.

_____ . "Jackson in the Shenandoah." *West Virginia History* 27 (January 1966): 85-96. West Virginia Department of Archives and History, Charleston, WV.

_____ . *General Turner Ashby and Stonewall's Valley Campaign*. Parsons WV: McClain Printing Co., 1980.

Catton, Bruce. *Glory Road*. Garden City NY: Doubleday and Co., 1952.

_____ . *A Stillness at Appomattox*. Garden City NY: Doubleday and Co., 1953.

_____ . *The Coming Fury*. Garden City NY: Doubleday and Co., 1961.

_____ . *The Centennial History of the Civil War*. Garden City NY: Doubleday and Co., 1978.

Chambers, Lenoir. *Stonewall Jackson*. Two volumes. New York: William Morrow and Co., 1959.

Chambers, Robert W. *Secret Service Operator 13*. New York: D. Appleton-Century Co., 1934.

Channing, Edward. *The War for Southern Independence. History of the United States*. Volume 6. New York: Macmillan Co., 1925.

Chestnut, Mary Boykin. *A Diary from Dixie*. Edited by Ben Ames Williams. New York: Houghton Mifflin and Co., 1947.

Chitwood, Oliver P., R. W. Patrick, and Frank L. Owsley. *The American People, A History*. Volume 1, third edition. Princeton: D. Van Nostrand Co., 1962.

Cooke, John Esten. *Wearing of the Gray*. New York: E. B. Treat and Co., 1867.

Coulter, E. M. *The Confederate States of America, 1861-65. History of the South.* Volume 7. Baton Rouge LA: Louisiana State University Press, 1950.

Craven, A. O. *A History of the South, 1848-67.* Volume 6. Baton Rouge LA: Louisiana State University Press, 1953.

Current, Richard N., T. Harry Williams, and Frank Friedel. *American History: A Survey.* Volume 1, to 1877. Fifth edition. New York: Alfred A. Knopf, 1979.

Davis, Burke. *Our Incredible Civil War.* New York: Holt, Rinehart, and Winston, 1960.

Davis, Curtis Carroll. "The Most Overrated Spy." Book review in *Southern Literary Messenger*, February 1942.

———. "The Most Overrated Spy." Book review in *Martinsburg* [WV] *Evening Journal*, 2 April 1942.

———. "The Civil War's Most Overrated Spy." *West Virginia Historical Quarterly* 27:12 (October 1965): 1-9. West Virginia Department of Archives and History. Charleston, WV.

———. *Belle Boyd in Camp and Prison.* Cranbury NJ: Thomas Yoseloff, 1968.

DeLeon, T. C. *Four Years in Rebel Capitals.* Mobile AL: Gossip Printing Co., 1890.

Dodd, William E. *The Cotton Kingdom, A Chronicle of the Old South.* Chronicles of America Series, edited by Allen Johnson, volume 27. New Haven CT: Yale University Press, 1919.

Doster, William E. *Lincoln and Episodes of the Civil War.* New York: G. P. Putnam's Sons, 1915.

Douglas, Henry Kyd. *I Rode With Stonewall.* Chapel Hill NC: University of North Carolina Press, 1940.

Dufour, Charles L. *Gentle Tiger, The Gallant Life of Roberdeau Wheatby.* Baton Rouge LA: Louisiana State University Press, 1957.

Eaton, Clement. *A History of the Southern Confederacy.* New York: Macmillan, 1954.

Evans, Willis F. *History of Berkeley County, West Virginia.* Printed privately, 1928.

Fish, Carl Russel. *The Development of American Nationality.* New York: American Book Co., 1922.

Freeman, Douglas Southall. *Lee's Lieutenants.* Volume 1. New York: Charles Scribner's Sons, 1942.

———. *Robert E. Lee, A Biography.* New York: Charles Scribner's Sons, 1947.

Gilmor, Harry. *Four Years In the Saddle*. London: Longmans Green and Co., 1866.

Glenn, James. Will of James Glenn. Charles Town WV: Will Book number 7.

Goldsborough, Euphemia. Diary, 1861-1865. Summit Point WV: owned by Mrs. Stuart Crimm.

Gordon, Nancy B. "Belle Boyd, The Confederate Spy." *The Southern Literary Messenger* 4:2 (February 1942): 66-74. Richmond VA: The Dietz Press.

Hale, Laura Virginia. *Belle Boyd, Southern Spy of the Shenandoah*. Front Royal VA: United Daughters of the Confederacy, Warren Rifles Chapter, 1936 (pamphlet).

_____ . *Four Valiant Years in the Lower Shenandoah Valley, 1861-65*. Strasburg VA: Shenandoah Publishing Co., 1968.

Harlow, Ralph V. *The Growth of the United States*. New York: Henry Holt and Co., 1932.

Henderson, George F. R. *Stonewall Jackson and the American Civil War*. New York: Longmans, Green and Co., 1936.

Hergesheimer, Joseph. *Swords and Roses*. New York: Alfred A. Knopf, 1929.

Horan, James D. *Desperate Women*. New York: G. P. Putnam's Sons, 1952.

Johnson, Allen, and Dumas Malone, editors. *Dictionary of American Biography*. New York: Charles Scribner's Sons, 1943. (Belle Boyd, p. 524.)

Jones, Catherine M. *Heroines of Dixie*. First edition. New York: The Bobbs-Merrill Co., 1955.

Kane, Harnett T. *Spies for the Blue and Gray*. Garden City NY: Hanover House, 1954.

_____ . *The Smiling Rebel*. Garden City NY: Doubleday, 1955 (novel).

Kenamond, A. D. [Article on Glenn Burnie]. *Jefferson County Historical Society Magazine* 29 (December 1963): 13-25. Charles Town WV: Jefferson Publishing Co.

Kerbey, Joseph O. *The Boy Spy: A Substantially True Record of Secret Service During the War of the Rebellion*. Chicago: American Mutual Library Association, 1889.

Lamon, Ward Hill. *Recollections of Abraham Lincoln, 1847-65*. Edited by Dorothy Lamon. Chicago: A. C. McClurg and Co., 1895.

Lawrence, George A. *Border and Bastille*. New York: W. I. Pooley and Co., 1863.

Leech, Margaret. *Reveille in Washington, 1860-1865*. New York: Harper and Brothers, 1941.

Long, E. B. and Barbara Long. *The Civil War Day by Day, an Almanac 1861-1865.* New York: Doubleday and Co., 1971.

MacDonald, Mary Ella. [Article on Belle Boyd.] *Wonderful West Virginia* 43:5 (July 1979). Charleston WV: West Virginia Department of Natural Resources.

Mahony, Dennis A. *The Prisoner of State.* New York: G. W. Carlton and Co., 1863.

Marshall, John A. *American Bastille.* Philadelphia: Thomas W. Hartley, 1872.

Massey, Mary E. *Bonnet Brigades.* New York: 1966.

McDonald, A. P., editor. *Make Me A Map of the Valley—The Civil War Journal of Stonewall Jackson's Topographer.* Dallas: Southern Methodist University Press, 1973.

McDonald, William N. *A History of the Laurel Brigade.* Edited by Bushrod Washington. Baltimore: Mrs. Kate S. McDonald (Sun Printing Co.), 1907.

McGuire, Mrs. J. W. *Diary of A Southern Refugee.* New York: E. G. Hale and Son, 1868.

Milton, John. *Paradise Lost.* (Various printings.)

Morrison, Samuel Eliot, and Henry Steele Commager. *The Growth of the American Republic.* Volume 1. Fifth edition. New York: Oxford University Press, 1962.

Morton, O. Frederick. *The History of Winchester in Virginia.* Strasburg VA: Shenandoah Publishing House, 1925.

Nevins, Allan. *Ordeal of the Union.* New York: Charles Scribner's Sons, 1947.

Norris, J. E. *A History of the Lower Shenandoah Valley.* Volume 1. Chicago: Warner and Co., 1890.

Owsley, Frank L. *King Cotton Diplomacy, Foreign Relations of the Confederate States of America.* Chicago: University of Chicago Press, 1931.

Pollard, Edward A. *Observations in the North.* Richmond VA: E. W. Ayres Co., 1865.

_____ . *The Lost Cause.* New York: Bonanza Books, n.d. (A facsimile of the original 1867 edition.)

Pratt, Fletcher. *Stanton, Lincoln's Secretary of War.* New York: Norton Press, 1953.

Quarles, Garland R. *Occupied Winchester, 1861-65.* Winchester VA: prepared for Farmers and Merchants Bank, 1976.

Randall, James G., and David Donald. *The Civil War and Reconstruction.* Second edition. Boston: D. C. Heath and Co., 1961.

Rhodes, James Ford. *History of the United States From the Compromise of 1850 to the Final Restoration of Home Rule at the South in 1877.* Volume 1 (1850-1854), and Volume 2 (1854-1860). New York: Macmillan Co., 1907.

Robertson, James I., Jr. *The Stonewall Brigade.* Baton Rouge LA: Louisiana State University Press, 1963.

Sampson, Anna Eliza. *Kith and Kin.* Richmond VA: The William Byrd Press, 1922.

Sandburg, Carl. *Abraham Lincoln, the War Years.* Volume 1. New York: Harcourt, Brace and Co., 1939.

Sigaud, Louis A. *Belle Boyd, Confederate Spy.* Second edition. Richmond VA: The Dietz Press, 1944.

_____ . "When Belle Boyd Wrote Lincoln." *Lincoln Herald* 50:1 (February 1948): 15-22. Harrogate TN: Lincoln Memorial University Press.

_____ . "Belle Boyd Immortalized." *United Daughters of the Confederacy Magazine* 16:9 (September 1953): 26-29.

_____ . "More About Belle Boyd." *Lincoln Herald* 64:4 (Winter 1962): 174-81. Harrogate TN: Lincoln Memorial University Press.

_____ . "William Boyd Compton: Belle Boyd's Cousin." *Lincoln Herald* 67 (Spring 1963): 22-33. Harrogate TN: Lincoln Memorial University Press.

Simkins, Francis B., and James W. Patton. *The Women of the Confederacy.* St. Clair Shores MI: Scholarly Press, 1977.

Stackpole, Edward J. *Sheridan in the Shenandoah.* Harrisburg PA: Stackpole Co., 1961.

Steiner, Bernard C. *History of Education in Maryland.* Washington DC: U. S. Government Printing Office, 1894.

Stephenson, Nathaniel W. *The Day of the Confederacy—A Chronicle of the Embattled South.* Volume 30. New Haven: Yale University Press, 1920.

Stern, Philip Van Doren. *Secret Missions of the Civil War.* New York: Bonanza Books, 1959.

Stevens, W. D. *The Shenandoah and Its Byways.* New York: Dodd, Mead and Co., 1941.

Stevenson, James Hunter. *Boots and Saddles: A History of the First Volunteer Cavalry of the War. Known as the First New York (Lincoln) Cavalry. . . .* Harrisburg PA: Patriot Publishing Co., 1879.

Strother, David Hunter. *A Virginia Yankee in the Civil War—The Diaries of David Hunter Strother.* Edited by Cecil H. Eby. Chapel Hill NC: University of North Carolina Press, 1961.

Taylor, Richard. *Destruction and Reconstruction.* New York: D. Appleton and Co., 1879.

Thomas, Emory M. *The Confederate Nation, 1861-65.* American Nation Series, edited by Henry Steele Commager and R. B. Moons. New York: Harper & Row, 1979.

Trefousse, Hans L. *Ben Butler—The South Called Him Beast*. New York: Octagon Books (Farrar, Strauss, and Giroux), 1974.

U. S. Navy Department. *Official Records of the Union and Confederate Navies in the War of the Rebellion 1894-1919*. Washington DC: U. S. Government Printing Office.

U.S. War Department. *Official Records of the Union and Confederate Armies in the War of the Rebellion, 1880-1901*. Washington DC: U. S. Government Printing Office.

Vandiver, Frank E. *Mighty Stonewall*. New York: McGraw-Hill Co., 1957.

Wayland, John W. *Virginia Valley Records. . . .* Strasburg VA: Shenandoah Publishing Co., 1930.

Wayland, J. W. *Stonewall Jackson's Way*. Staunton VA: McClure Co., 1940.

Weston, B. Latrobe. "The Story of Mt. Washington, Md." *Maryland Historical Magazine* 43:36 (March 1948). Baltimore: Maryland Historical Society.

Wiley, B. I. *Confederate Women*. Westport CT: Greenwood Press, 1975.

Williams, T. Harry. *P. G. T. Beauregard—Napoleon in Gray*. Baton Rouge LA: Louisiana State University Press, 1955.

Williamson, James J. *Prison Life in the Old Capitol and Reminiscences of the Civil War*. West Orange NJ: 1911.

Willis, Carrie Hunter, and Etta Belle Walker. *Legends of the Skyline Drive and of the Great Valley of Virginia*. Richmond VA: The Dietz Press, 1937.

LIBRARIES CONSULTED

Fairmont State College Library, Fairmont WV.
Handley Memorial Library, Winchester VA.
Lawson McGhee Library, McClung Historical Room, Knoxville TN.
Library of Congress, Washington DC.
Martinsburg Public Library, Martinsburg WV.
Samuels Library, Front Royal VA.
Shepherd College Library, Shepherdstown WV.
University of Tennessee (Main Library), Knoxville TN.
West Virginia University Library, Morgantown WV.

Index

MP BELLE BOYD, SIREN OF THE SOUTH

Designed by Haywood Ellis

Composition by Omni Composition Services
the text was "read" by a Hendrix Typereader II OCR Scanner
and formatted on an Addressograph Multigraph Comp/Set 5404,
then paginated on an A/M Comp/Set 4510.

Production specifications:
text paper — 60 pound Warren's Olde Style
end papers — Multicolor Antique Russet
cover (on .088 boards) — Holliston Roxite A 49241, die stamped
with Kurz-Hastings Colorit 912
dustjacket — 100 pound enamel, printed three colors (PMS 322, PMS 145,
and black), and varnished

Printing (offset lithography) by Omnipress of Macon, Inc., Macon, Georgia
Binding by John H. Dekker and Sons, Inc., Grand Rapids, Michigan